The Provost's House Stables
Building & Environs, Trinity College Dublin

Published on behalf of TRIARC – Irish Art Research Centre,
Trinity College Dublin, by

Æ

ASSOCIATED EDITIONS

Æ

ASSOCIATED EDITIONS

Published on the occasion of
the official launch of
The Provost's House Stables, Trinity College Dublin
12 June 2008

This edition © 2008 Associated Editions Ltd
Text © 2008 TRIARC - Irish Art Research Centre, Dublin and the authors

First published in 2008
by Associated Editions Ltd
33 Melrose Avenue
Dublin 3
Ireland
www.associatededitions.ie

on behalf of:

TRIARC - Irish Art Research Centre
Department of the History of Art
School of Histories and Humanities
Trinity College Dublin
Dublin 2
Ireland
www.triarc.ie
tel + 353 1 896 3176
fax + 353 1896 1438
email triarc@tcd.ie
website www.triarc.ie

ISBN: 978 -1 -906429- 01 -0

Book Editors: Yvonne Scott and Rachel Moss
Copy Editor: Elizabeth Mayes
Book design: Anne Brady, Vermillion Design
Printed in Ireland

CONTENTS

PREFACE

Yvonne Scott, Director

It is less than five years since the Trinity Irish Art Research Centre (TRIARC) opened its metaphorical doors to the first group of eager students and researchers, keen to expand their understanding of the history of Irish art and architecture. This development was a response to the expanding international recognition of Irish visual culture of all periods, and consequent demand for opportunities for education and research in the field. This publication celebrates the official opening of its *actual* doors – giving entry into the newly restored Provost's House Stables, a building that has been sensitively renovated by award-winning architects, O'Donnell+Tuomey, to provide a permanent home for the Centre. The Centre is an integral part of the History of Art Department in the School of Histories and Humanities, Trinity College Dublin, and it has the benefit of exploiting the well-established expertise in Irish art and architecture that has characterised the Department since its foundation by Anne Crookshank forty years ago.

The idea for a research centre dedicated to Irish art originated with Anne's successor as Chair, Roger Stalley. In association with Mary Apied, President of the Trinity Foundation, he also secured the initial funding. This enabled, first, the appointment of a director to take overall responsibility and to co-ordinate a post-graduate programme, and, subsequently, a second post was created to look after the visual archive and contribute to teaching. The last four to five years have been exciting and busy: laying the foundation of the academic and research programme and attracting a body of good students; in hosting a series of seminars, symposia and conferences; in establishing a series of published research; in initiating the cataloguing and digitisation of the extensive and unique visual archive (initially comprising the Crookshank-Glin, Stalley, and Rae collections); in cataloguing and expanding the collection of books on Irish art that were generously donated to the Centre by Prof. Crookshank; and of course continuing to work with the Foundation to ensure the future viability of the endeavour. In addition, funding to carry out various research projects was sought and achieved from sources including

Opposite: The Provost's House Stables. View from the cobbled courtyard.

The Getty Foundation, the Irish Research Council for the Humanities and Social Sciences (IRCHSS), and the Heritage Council.

Soon after its inception, it became evident that if the concept of a Centre was to be a practical reality, a dedicated location would be vital, and the defunct Stables building – empty since the departure of the horses – proved the ideal solution. A generous benefaction enabled this idea to become a reality – for a hay loft to transform into a reading room, a carriage house to convert to a seminar room, for horse stalls to translate into study carrels, in short – for a stables block to metamorphose into a centre for academic research.

The essays in this volume explore the Provost's House Stables building and its immediate environs. Following a preface by Desmond FitzGerald, Knight of Glin, the first two essays, by Edward McParland and by John Tuomey, respectively, record and consider, first, the original design of the building and, then, the philosophy of its recent restoration for a different, but equally practical, purpose. These are followed by a lively exposition by Patricia McCarthy on the design and use of stables generally in Ireland up to the time the Trinity College Stables building was erected. As you walk along the path towards the Stables building, off to the left is an ancient well, part of a water system that gave Nassau Street its original name of St Patrick's Well Lane, and Rachel Moss unearths its fascinating history. Finally, a brief essay interprets the new sculpture by Michael Warren, dedicated to Samuel Beckett to mark the centenary of his birth. This work was donated to the College by David Arnold, and it has been installed in the cobbled yard, turned as though to point the way toward the Stables.

This group of essays, in representing various periods, from the medieval to the present, in examining various different forms of visual culture, and in being written by both art historians and practitioners, gives some indication of the wide range that falls within the ambit of the Centre.

The launch of the Provost's House Stables is a turning point, marking the completion of the foundation phase to establish the Centre. We look forward to the next phase, of bringing projects to fruition and instigating opportunities, and of welcoming students and researchers to pursue their exploration of Irish art history in what we hope will prove a conducive and collegial environment.

ACKNOWLEDGEMENTS

We are deeply grateful to Clare and Tony White whose generous sponsorship supported the publication of this book. We extend special thanks to all of the contributors to the book for their well-researched, scholarly, and absorbing essays. Thanks also to the many associates who supported the writers in their research with their comments and direction, and also to the various research institutions whose collections have yielded much of the primary and secondary material referred to in the essays. These have been acknowledged by the individual writers in their footnotes, and in their notes of thanks. Grateful thanks are extended to all who gave images and copyright permissions, enabling this book to be so extensively illustrated.

Mary Apied, President of the Trinity Foundation, and her colleagues there have provided vital support, for which we are deeply grateful.

Anne Brady and her team at Vermillion provided their customary excellent design and publication service, and Elizabeth Mayes contributed invaluable copy-editing and proof-reading assistance.

Finally, heartfelt thanks to a special friend of Trinity College whose exceptional generosity supported the restoration of this significant building and thereby provided a place for learning – and the *raison d'être* for this book.

Yvonne Scott and *Rachel Moss* (editors)

INTRODUCTION
Desmond FitzGerald, Knight of Glin

Wandering along Nassau Street, I often wondered what the reserved, classically ordered, unwindowed granite structure sequestered behind the magnificent high College railings was used for (fig.1). I never knew until recently that this was the street façade of the Provost's House Stables. What a transformation has taken place to this once forgotten and dilapidated space. Now the interiors are transformed into sympathetic research and teaching spaces. The original horse stalls of the stables are converted into spacious study carrels for postgraduate students. The original granite floor retains the old gulleys and drainage channels, with services like heating hidden from sight, so the integrity of the building is faithfully maintained. Elsewhere there is a well-equipped seminar room, a research room for digitisation projects, and a reading room stocked with art-historical books and the TRIARC Archive of Irish art images. This extensive photographic holding consists of four significant collections. Prof. Roger Stalley's collection comprises more than 20,000 original photographs of Irish medieval architecture and sculpture, taken by him over almost four decades, and providing the tools for his many learned books and articles. Another medieval grouping is the Edwin Rae collection of photographs of medieval tomb sculpture, wayside crosses and Irish architecture. This significant tradition is being developed and expanded by Rachel Moss who also, as Archive Manager, is overseeing the cataloguing and digitisation of the collection. This vital project will make the entire collection more accessible to all. The burgeoning Modern and Contemporary collection, being assembled by Yvonne Scott, will add substantially to the Archive.

However, the largest of the collections at present is the Crookshank-Glin comprising photographic images of Irish painting from the sixteenth to the early twentieth centuries. This represents the fruits of our forty years work and it used to be housed in Prof. Anne Crookshank's rooms in the Rubrics not far away across Trinity's main square. It was there that Anne and I wrote our three books and many articles on the Irish art of this period. The room was something of a crucible for the exploration of what was, in those days, an underdeveloped field. How well I remember the arguments and heated discussions we had as Anne pecked away at

Opposite: *Fig. 1* – Provost's House Stables. Street Façade. Photo, Ros Kavanagh.

the computer over those many years! It was Anne who was the first lecturer in Art History and founder of the Department at Trinity College. It was her enthusiasm, determination and sense of humour that inspired us all, and her memorable voice still echoes in my ears. The Provost's House Stables are, in a way, a culmination of a brilliant tradition conceived by her generous vision. A friend has written that Anne's room was a place where everyone in the field was made welcome and there was always an open door policy for anyone investigating Irish art, whether or not they had a formal connection with the College. Many people came in and out and chatted about their thoughts and discoveries and delved into our photographic boxes. This sharing was a generous exchange of information and her room was very much an embryonic research centre over the years before it was replaced by TRIARC in these beautifully renovated and adapted stables. I am sure that this new environment will continue the hospitable tradition made so familiar by the redoubtable Anne in that Rubrics room.

This new Trinity resource dovetails brilliantly with the recently created National Gallery Centre for the Study of Irish Art further down Nassau Street. To underline that dovetailing, it is Brendan Rooney who now heads up the Centre, who worked with Anne and me during all those years of research for our book *Ireland's Painters*. He is ably assisted by Donal Maguire, a postgraduate student with TRIARC. It is also well worth mentioning the superb library facilities specialising in Irish art at the National Irish Visual Art Library (NIVAL), at the National College of Art and Design not far away. These three facilities provide an unparalleled resource in central Dublin for historians and critics of Irish art.

In addition, TRIARC, and the History of Art Department to which it belongs, provide a unique range of courses at all levels and a postgraduate programme devoted to Irish Art History. Their brief also encompasses a programme of excellent seminars, symposia and conferences, and these, together with a series of publications and articles devoted to Irish art, are all designed to bring the latest academic research and lively commentaries to a receptive audience.

This, the latest TRIARC publication, commemorates its opening, and mention must be made of the five important essays that the book contains. Edward McParland's ingenious discussion memorialises the architect Frederick Darley's stables building which was completed in 1844. It examines the somewhat austere design of the stables, and puts them in context with their location on Nassau Street, leading on to Merrion Square and the road to Kingstown. The impressive College railings, or 'grille', by Robert Mallet is fully charted, along with Darley's own biography as College architect. This is followed by the story of the conversion of the stables and its refurbishment by the architect John Tuomey, who responds sensitively to the original design. The haylofts and rooms for grooms and coachmen now house the reading room and archive, and the eager students working there, while the horse stalls and carriage rooms provide study and seminar spaces. The O'Donnell+Tuomey design improves the daylight in the rooms without in any way compromising the building.

Patricia McCarthy then gives us an in-depth, magisterial history of the types and uses of Irish stables from the seventeenth to nineteenth centuries – so suitable for the commemoration of the Provost's stables. This ground-breaking material reveals the hitherto unexplored social history of this common building type. Vast amounts of money were expended on stable designs, ensuring the wellbeing of the owners' horses. Riding, hunting and racing were the constant pursuit of Ireland's nobility and gentry and frequently their stables were far grander than their country houses. Patricia's work on stables and farm buildings might be the subject of continued research. So often the big house has been destroyed or burnt but the offices remain.

The final two essays, by Rachel Moss and Yvonne Scott, examine aspects of the environs of the Stables, telling respectively the story of St Patrick's Well, traditionally thought to be located in a vault under the Nassau Street entrance to the College and, in contrast, the new Michael Warren sculpture commemorating Samuel Beckett, and located in the cobbled stable yard. The well was an ancient focal point for the revelry that took place on St Patrick's Day, and Rachel explores its history from the twelfth century to the present day. Yvonne Scott investigates the intriguing relationship between Warren's sculpture, *Go deo: homage to Samuel Beckett*, and Beckett's famous tragicomedy *Waiting for Godot*. Appropriately, both Warren and Beckett are former students of the College.

The commemoration of the renewal of the Provost's House Stables, to house TRIARC, in this book of essays is a milestone in the encouragement of the study of the history of Irish art and I like to think of Anne Crookshank's toiling in this field as a seminal influence on its creation.

THE PROVOST'S HOUSE STABLES, TRINITY COLLEGE DUBLIN

Edward McParland

Fig. 1 – The Provost's House Stables, south front to Nassau Street. Photo, the author.

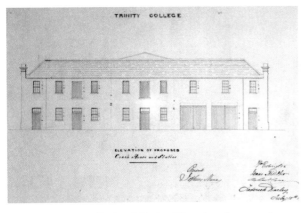

Fig. 2 – Frederick Darley, 'Elevation of proposed Coach House and Stables', showing the north front as proposed in July1841. Dublin City Library and Archive, Pearse Street, WSC/Maps/190/2.

First, some facts. The Provost's House Stables in Trinity College Dublin (fig. 1) were designed by the architect Frederick Darley junior (1798–1872). Immediately south of the Provost's House, they are on the corner of Grafton Street and Nassau Street, behind a tall granite wall and cast iron railing which divide Nassau Street from the College Park. Work started on stables and wall in 1842; on 20 January 1844 the Board of the College received information from the late Lord Mayor of a vote of thanks to the Provost and Board 'for their recent improvement of Nassau Street'.[1]

It is a shallow building, one bay deep, with a nine-bay south façade facing Nassau Street. Its two short sides are also of granite and, like the street front, are devoid of openings (except for one window low down on the east front). Street front and sides are articulated by pilasters, the mouldings of which are Greek rather than Roman. The pilasters on the street front carry a horizontal entablature, above which a parapet rises in steps to the central bay. One feels that this central bay needs a crowning element: a coat of arms, perhaps, or a chimney stack masquerading as an urn. The rendered façade facing the Provost's House (fig. 2) is less formal, but a little more revealing about the purpose of the building.

It is not a building that draws attention to itself. Its design is reticent, even austere. Its urban manners are good, its granite façades facing outwards to the city carrying a classical ordonnance, while its front to the College is of rendered brick. Further, it is partly framed by trees, and – more effectively – by John and Robert Mallet's high railings which are set less than four feet in front of it. These carry the eye beyond it to the east for well over 1,000 feet. And Darley, the College architect, was not a Richard Morrison, or a Benjamin Woodward: his work elsewhere in the College is also reticent. Given his talents, that is just as well.

Why, then, is the story of the erection of Darley's building so interesting?

The answer, of course, is that issues wider than the comfort of the Provost's horses, or the architect's skill, were involved. If we take the documents at face value, the initiative came from a source no less elevated than the Lord Lieutenant. Some years

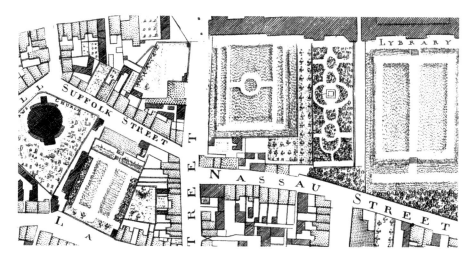

later, Daniel O'Connell was dragged in, when the affair became the subject of contentious legislation in Westminster. The ramifications of the architect's family – academic and legal as well as architectural – offer a fascinating vignette of nineteenth-century Dublin. And anyone who admires the stupendous line of wall and railings in Nassau Street soon comes to realise that the Provost's House Stables are an integral part of one of the greatest surviving monuments of the Wide Streets Commissioners' town planning: the Commissioners, not the College, provided the money for the work.

The key to the significance of the building is in its location, at the west end of Nassau Street where it joins Grafton Street. That is where the earlier stable building had been, narrowing (together with its neighbouring houses) the mouth of Nassau Street. John Rocque, an unusually reliable witness, shows the site in 1756 (fig. 3): the Provost's House is not yet built, and Nassau Street, at about forty feet wide, is not quite aligned with Suffolk Street. The buildings on the north (College) side of the western end of Nassau Street are, as shown by Rocque, at least partly believable: the projection of the most westerly one (then No.1 Grafton Street) beyond the western boundary of the College is confirmed in later maps (e.g. fig. 4), and the hatching, rather than stippling, of some of the buildings, which are roughly on the site of the present Provost's House Stables, indicates, in Rocque's legend, warehouses or stables.

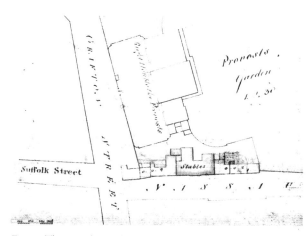

Fig. 4 – Thomas Sherrard, 'A survey of Part of the City of Dublin…' (1781). Detail showing the same corner of Nassau Street and Grafton Street as fig. 3. TCD Library, MUN/MC/11. ©The Board of Trinity College Dublin.

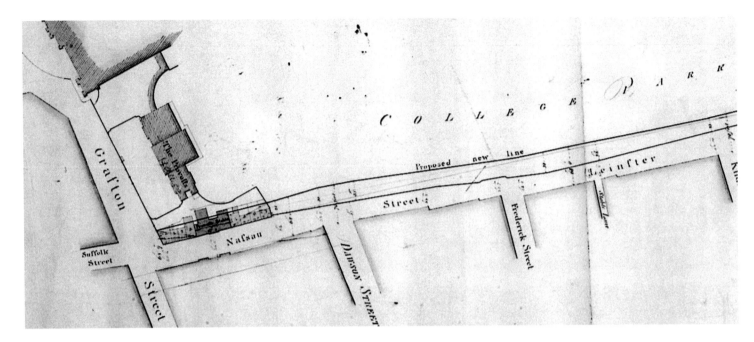

Fig. 5 – Thomas Sherrard, 'Map of Nassau Street…' (1833). Detail. Note the 'Proposed new line' to the College Park, with the existing line in ink to the south. Faintly visible between these lines is a pencil line representing the College's proposal for widening the street while keeping the houses and stables at the western end. Dublin City Library and Archive, Pearse Street, WSC/Maps/632.

Twenty-five years later, the footprint of these buildings on the corner of Nassau Street and Grafton Street had changed (fig. 4). No.1 Grafton Street still projects into the street in front of the College boundary: James Malton implied that it had been cleared away by the early 1790s. But, flanked by neighbouring houses, a building identified as the Provost's House Stables has assumed the plan of the building which was the one replaced by Darley in the 1840s.

The year 1833 is a good one in which to take up the story of the present Provost's House Stables. There, in a map of the Wide Streets Commissioners of that year, is the older building, soon to be replaced (fig. 5). It has a street frontage of sixty-seven feet, and some formality is suggested by its central breakfront. Otherwise, nothing is known about it, though what seem to be remains of these earlier stables were found in excavations connected with recent work on the site (fig. 6). As to other early stables in the College, a range of building west of the Dining Hall shown in Samuel Byron's bird's-eye view of 1780 can be identified from other maps as stables (fig. 7). At this time there were stables, too, beside the bowling green at the east end of the College.

This map of 1833 (fig. 5) reveals much of the thinking about the site at that time. By the 1830s Nassau Street, the main approach to Merrion Square from the centre of the city, needed improvement, not least because, beyond Merrion Square, it led to the fast-developing harbour at Kingstown, now Dun Laoghaire. And so, in 1833, the Under-Secretary William Gosset represented to the Wide Streets Commissioners that the Lord Lieutenant favoured the widening of the street: for a work of such 'urgent necessity', he wrote, it was 'not improbable that the Members of the Board of Fellows of Trinity College might be induced to grant a few feet of the College Garden along the Dead Wall which separates it from Nassau and Lienster [*sic*] streets… at a very trifling sacrifice to themselves… the greatly increased thoroughfare from the corner of Nassau Street through Merrion Square, in consequence of the new opening into the Kingstown Road, seems to point out the improvement as not only desirable but also as an object of urgent necessity'. [2] Only speculation can assist in seeking the reason for interest in the road to Kingstown Harbour, and beyond, on the part of the Lord Lieutenant, the Marquess of Anglesey.

It was only to be expected that negotiations for those 'few feet' would be protracted. It was clearly going to be much simpler for the Wide Streets Commissioners to widen the street towards the north, where – apart from those with interests in the houses at the western end – there was only a single proprietor to deal with for the land in the College Park. Hence the 'Proposed new line' of Sherrard's map of 1833: demolish the old Provost's Stables and the few neighbouring houses, take a strip – up to thirty-eight feet wide – off the College Park, and erect a new boundary in a more or less straight line as far as Park Street (now Lincoln Place). We can see the original boundary to the park on this map. And diagonal lines from the street-front corners of the stables, when read together with a pencil line proposing pulling back the fronts of the buildings between Grafton and Dawson Streets, imply suggestions for widening the mouth of Nassau Street by demolishing the houses beside the stables, but not the stables themselves.

In December 1833 the College determined to oppose the demolition of the stables and houses and any application for an act of parliament that would alienate College land, and to build a new boundary wall from the corner of Goodison's house (the most easterly one) in a straight line as far as Lincoln Place, but only when the Commissioners had widened the whole street on the other side. [3] The College's

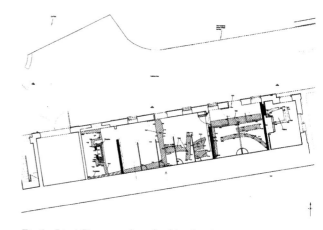

Fig. 6 – Linzi Simpson, plan of stables showing (hatched) remains of earlier structures; the deep south wall represents the plan at podium level, deep enough to carry the iron railings. For Margaret Gowen & Co Ltd, 'Archaeological monitoring of the Provost's Stables… for Trinity College Dublin', Unpublished report, 2007.

Fig. 7 – Samuel Byron, Isometric view of the College (1780). Detail. Shown to the left of the Dining Hall, entered from a yard in College Street, is a stable building. TCD Library, MUN/MC/9. ©The Board of Trinity College Dublin.

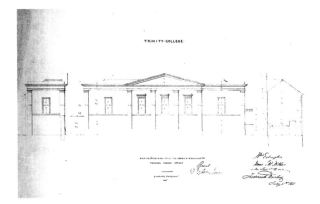

Fig. 8 – Frederick Darley, 'Elevation for the proposed stables…', showing the main south front to Nassau Street as proposed in July 1841. Dublin City Library and Archive, Pearse Street, WSC/Maps/190/1.

proposed line of compromise is shown as the faint pencil line of fig. 5 between the existing boundary, and the 'Proposed new line' of the Commissioners.

In 1837 the College was still fighting its corner to preserve stables and houses (it had shared interests in the houses). But in that year the Commissioners were preparing to play their winning card. They had always enjoyed the power to purchase compulsorily the properties needed for their street-widening plans. A private bill was introduced to enable them to remove the houses at the Grafton Street corner, 'together with the Provost's Stables, and… [to take in] so much of the College Park as will increase the Width of the Street to Seventy Feet'.[4] The Commissioners solicited Daniel O'Connell to support the bill; the College instructed its representatives in parliament to oppose it.[5] The result was a compromise: the Commissioners could take land from the College, but not without the consent of the Provost and Fellows.[6] The bill received royal assent on 15 July 1837.

'Consent', of course, meant compensation. After four years of haggling the College settled: for £10,223 from the Commissioners, the College agreed to sacrifice its interest in the houses beside the old stables, to yield the land from its park necessary to widening the street, and to build new stables and a new wall with railings the length of Nassau Street.[7]

On 10 July 1841 the Commissioners, with Darley, signed drawings for the work (figs. 2, 8, 9, 10). From these we see the plan (fig. 9) substantially as executed (though with eight stalls and no loose boxes). The stable yard is approached both from Grafton Street (through a gate that survived until *c.*1920, when the College ceded to the Corporation land at the corner of Nassau and Grafton Streets to accommodate traffic) and from the yard in front of the Provost's House. The rear façade (fig. 2) is also much as executed. The street façade (fig. 8) is, however, something of a mystery, as it is about twenty feet shorter than both the front to the yard and the street front as shown on the plan signed by the Commissioners at the same time (fig. 9). Further, the street façade of the plan, unlike that of fig. 8, has two bays on either side of the breakfront instead of one, and a niche in each of the three central bays.

About this time, Darley was persuaded to propose economies to the design he had been preparing, and it seems as if he had rushed out a new simplified (and inaccurate) façade design (fig. 8) without having time to revise the plan.[8] The Wide

Streets Commissioners' minutes speak of how he proposed omitting the rustication (probably on the base of the street front) and also the concave niches.[9] Basement rustication was rendered superfluous when it was agreed to continue the wall and railings in front of the stables.[10] But the difference in length between the front and back of the building is unexplained. Darley would have been aware of it – but maybe the signing ceremony was preceded by lunch.

A further oddity of these proposals is their inclusion, against the new park wall, but far to the east and facing the mouth of South Frederick Street, of a range of what are clearly water closets but are identified on the drawings as 'mews' (fig. 10). What seem to be personal water closets, each one with a locked door, are referred to as mews elsewhere in the College records at this time.[11] This use of the word 'mews' is unknown to the *Oxford English Dictionary*.

Darley's plan of July 1841 for the stables (fig. 9) provided on the ground floor for a coach house, two compartments of stalls (one for five, one for three horses), with a staircase at either end of the building. Upstairs there were haylofts above the stalls, and probably residential accommodation over the coach house. The haylofts were served on this front by separate storey-high opes to receive the hay, and four slatted

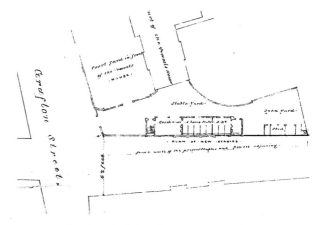

Fig. 9 – Frederick Darley, 'Plan of Nassau Street and Leinster Street…' (1841). Detail. Dublin City Library and Archive, Pearse Street, WSC/Maps/190/4.

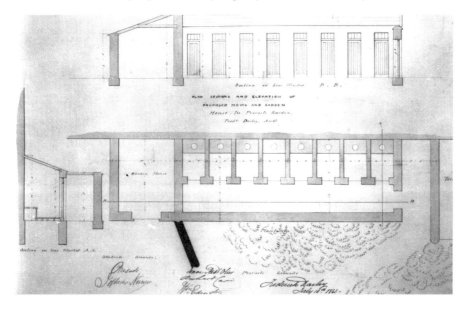

Fig. 10 – Frederick Darley, 'Plan sections and elevation of proposed mews…' (1841). Dublin City Library and Archive, Pearse Street, WSC/Maps/190/3.

Fig. 11 – O'Donnell+Tuomey Architects, ground plan of the stables before alteration (2005). Shading added by author. Note the deep south wall as in figure 6.

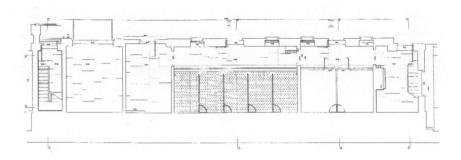

(probably unglazed) windows. Division of stalls into five and three, and separate provision aloft for delivery and storage of hay, sent by chute down to the stalls below, probably indicates that the Provost shared his stabling with others.

Darley's eight stalls of July 1841 do not correspond to the recently surviving accommodation, which allowed for five stalls and two loose boxes (fig. 11). Taken together, the two loose boxes are exactly the width of three stalls. Perhaps the loose boxes were Darley's idea: more probably they were a later alteration. Introduced to stable design in the late eighteenth century, the loose box suited the ailing horse, or the mare in foal, or the hunter fresh from sustained exercise in the field.[12] In terms of equine economy, Darley's design was conservative: there was no central drainage for the stalls, and little specific provision for ventilation, so perhaps the loose boxes, still something of an innovation in the early nineteenth century, were not his. (Hunting provosts once had to search further afield than their own garden, which nowadays is home to urban foxes).

There is no doubt that Darley's wall, and the railings affording views into College Park along the length of Nassau Street, are an important scenic contribution to the city centre street, all the more significant since cities such as London saw the loss to armaments of such monumental iron work during World War II (fig. 12). Articles of agreement were signed on 6 October 1842 between the College and the Mallets for erecting 1,290 feet of railing, with two wicket gates, for £1,323 10s. 0d. (fig. 13).[13] *The Irish Builder* gushed in 1869 that the railing was 'generally deemed one of the handsomest stretches of iron "grille" in Europe and certainly much better than anything that London presents'.[14] The railing is protective, but transparent, a more friendly barrier to the College than the 'Dead wall' which

Fig. 12 – Railings to the College Park, Nassau Street. Photo, the author.

preceded it. And as we have seen, the wall, railing and stable were conceived together, as an improvement of the avenue which led ultimately to Kingstown Harbour, and beyond.

Robert Mallet, born in 1810, was the more famous of the two, and joined his father John's foundry in Dublin on his return from a European tour in the early 1830s. [15] He soon took over the running of the foundry, relieving his father, who was much occupied on Dublin Corporation business. At the time of their work on the Nassau Street railings, they were also providing cast iron chain posts, and chains, to surround the College lawns. Robert, who had taken his BA degree in Trinity in 1830, rose to become President of the Institution of Civil Engineers of Ireland. Given the Mallets' triumph, it is curious that they were not employed when it was decided in 1845 to commission Courtney and Stephens to continue the railings into Grafton Street, 'on exactly the same plan and level as the part already erected….'. [16]

No one who was familiar with the ins and outs of society in Dublin in the early nineteenth century would have been surprised that the architect to the College was Frederick Darley junior. True, at about this time, the College was undoing the stonework of the Old Library which had been provided over a hundred years earlier from the Darley quarries in County Down (it had quickly begun to scale, and had to be entirely replaced in the nineteenth century). But Darleys had served the College as masons and stonecutters throughout the eighteenth century: Moses, Hugh (who was clerk of works for the building of the West Front of the College in the 1750s), Henry, and George. And by the 1820s, the family was distinguishing itself academically: our architect's brother was elected a Fellow in 1823 and, between 1820 and 1830, no fewer than twelve Darleys proceeded to a degree from Trinity. Frederick senior (though 'referred to in 1802 as being "among the most eminent architects of the kingdom…" would probably be more properly described as a developer'[17]) had consolidated the family position by marrying a Guinness and by becoming Lord Mayor in 1808–9. And the solicitor who handled the negotiations of the Wide Streets Commissioners with the College was a Henry Farran Darley. Frederick junior, therefore, had an hereditary claim to the commissions from the College in the 1830s to build two residential ranges which would form New Square, the little Magnetic Observatory (now moved to University College Dublin), and the Nassau Street wall and Provost's House Stables.

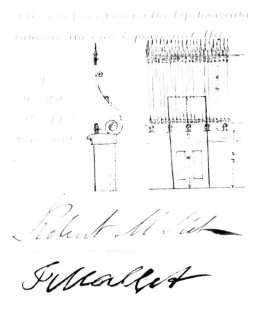

Fig. 13 – Articles of agreement between the College and Robert and John Mallet for the erection of railings, 6 October 1842. Detail. TCD Library, MUN/P2/303. ©The Board of Trinity College Dublin.

These were small, or utilitarian, buildings, and it is hard to fault their Spartan granite decency (the refinement of the Observatory derives from its use of Portland stone). The same is true of Darley's King's Inns Library in Henrietta Street, distinguished more by its learning – its Greek Doric portico is the earliest in Dublin – than by its imagination. When he got the opportunity to slip the leash, and to produce designs (unexecuted) for what is now the Museum Building in the College, the result was more pompous than grand.[18] Perhaps his wall and railings in Nassau Street which, in their extent, aspire to the monumental, are his best work.

Darley was trained by Francis Johnston, the architect of the General Post Office in Dublin and of the Chapel in Dublin Castle. Darley's own most prominent pupil was John McCurdy, to whom he passed on the job of architect to the College. His background in Johnston's office may have prepared the way for his stylistic eclecticism (many of his schools were Tudor Gothic), and for his reticent Hellenism. In a way that was more common in the late eighteenth, rather than in the nineteenth, century (though he was active into the 1860s), he was – in matters of style – a magpie.

So Darley comes at the end of Dublin's Georgian classicism, and though the tradition was continued and enlivened a little longer in the city (and elsewhere) by John Skipton Mulvany, the College was soon to allow Deane and Woodward, in their Museum Building, to complete Darley's Corinthian New Square with a radical Ruskinian alternative to the servile and pagan architecture of classicism.

It has been shown in this essay that the present Provost's House Stables played a part in the Wide Streets Commissioners' replanning of one of the major avenues leading from the centre of Dublin. To this improvement, the College surrendered about an acre of its park. As well as being widened, the rough causeway of Nassau Street was levelled. What was once St Patrick's Well Lane was now to be a thoroughfare of which no European city need be embarrassed. What was once a College boundary, described as a 'tottering… fence… [of] unsightly and inconveniently irregular shape'[19] was now a great cast iron palisade one quarter of a mile in length. And if the stables building itself comes at the end of a tradition, it was conceived as an integral part of a forward-looking approach to town planning which in Dublin, as elsewhere, was shaping our modern cities. And if it would be an exaggeration to talk, in the doing of all this, of valleys being exalted, or of mountains and hills being made low, at least all that levelling and straightening must have gladdened the Victorian mind: for the crooked had been made a little more straight, and the rough places a little more plain.

I am grateful to Sheila Carden and Mary McGrath for valuable assistance in preparing this essay. Figures 2, 5, 8, 9 and 10 appear with the permission of the Dublin City Library and Archive; figures 4, 7 and 13 with the permission of the Board of Trinity College; figure 11 with the permission of O'Donnell+Tuomey, Architects; figure 6 with permission of Margaret Gowan and Co. Ltd.

[1]   TCD Library, Registers of the Board, MUN/V/5/8 (20 Jan. 1844).

[2]   Dublin City Library and Archive, Pearse Street, Wide Streets Commissioners' Minutes. WSC/mins/ vol. 41 (15 May 1833).

[3]   TCD MUN/V/5/7 (23 Dec. 1833).

[4]   *An act to extend, alter, and enlarge, the powers of several acts for enabling the Commissioners of Wide Streets in Dublin, to widen and improve certain ways, streets, and passages…*, 1 Vic cap cxxvii (private).

[5]   WSC/mins/ vol. 43 (15 Feb. 1837, and 19 April, mistakenly referred to as February in the minutes, 1837).

[6]   WSC/mins/ vol. 43 (26 April, mistakenly referred to as July in the minutes,1837).

[7]   TCD MUN/V/5/8 (25 June 1842).

[8]   WSC/mins/ vol. 46 (14 July 1841).

[9]   *Ibid.*

[10]   TCD MUN/V/5/8 (4 Dec. 1842)

[11]   For example in TCD Library, the accounts of J. and R. Mallet, 1841 (MUN/P2/299/36).

[12]   Giles Worsley, *The British stable* (New Haven and London, 2004).

[13]   TCD Library, articles of agreement between J. and R. Mallet and the College, 6 Oct. 1842 (MUN/P2/303).

[14]   *The Irish Builder*, 1 June, 1869.

[15]   Ronald Cox (ed.), *Robert Mallet, FRS, 1810–1881* (Dublin, 1982).

[16]   TCD MUN/V/5/8 (22 April 1845).

[17]   Ann Martha Rowan (compiler), entries on the Darleys in 'Biographical index of Irish architects', database in The Irish Architectural Archive.

[18]   TCD Library, architectural drawings, 1833–7 (MUN/MC/85).

[19]   WSC/mins/ vol. 44 (8 May 1839).

TRANSLATION: IN SEARCH OF CHARACTER

John Tuomey

Fig. 1 – The stableyard resurfaced.
Photo, Ros Kavanagh

Although there are those who might deny it, and despite the levelling deluge of regulatory controls, it is arguable that an architect's job may not have changed very much in its scope, in its essence, or in its effect since Frederick Darley designed the Provost's House Stables in the early nineteenth century. By way of overture to this introduction to our own modest conversion of the stables (for researchers to study where horses once stood), it might be useful to consider a slightly earlier work by the same author to illustrate the common ground. Merchant's Arch (Frederick Darley, 1821) is a satisfyingly complex piece of urban architecture. It operates inside and outside of itself, both as building block and city passage. It faces north across the Liffey with solemn formality, a big three-windowed and rooflit room raised over an arcaded ground floor with a public archway carved through at one side. Completed ten years after the Ha'penny Bridge, it joins forces with the pedestrian bridge to connect the smaller scale backstreets to the grander scale of the Quays. It is not simply a stand-alone pavilion, but a more strategic mechanism, carefully assembled by someone who could read and relate to the wider context, who could answer the immediate requirements of development with a more reciprocal response that would integrate the various and potentially conflicting conditions of the given situation.

Twenty years later, Darley delivered a similarly well considered solution to the unlikely problem of accommodating the Provost's horses and carriages at the very visible and prominent street corner of Grafton Street with Trinity College. The Provost's House (John Smyth, 1759) presents a Palladian town house façade to Grafton Street and a plainer face to its gardens within the College grounds. In its eighteenth-century elevated certainty, Smyth's design calmly ignores the side issue of any relationship with the then built-up Nassau Street boundary. Frederick Darley made an interesting little exercise out of the combination of these conditions. He was no stranger to the situation, earlier generations of Darleys having provided stonecutting and site supervision for the Provost's House, and Darley himself, as official architect to the College, having already designed the Magnetic Observatory on axis with the Provost's House itself.

By blinding three outer faces of the four-sided stable block, then wrapping them over in a rhythm of Doric pilasters standing on a plain podium and carrying an attic entablature, the utilitarian nature of the building is concealed. The Greek Revival language of the façade represents the College to the city and contributes a closing compositional element to the otherwise exposed north side of the Provost's House itself.

To comply with the restrictive rules of this scheme, all but one of the normal and necessary openings for access, light and ventilation had to be collected on the non-public northern side, and on this elevation the high rhetoric of the (almost) windowless façades is dropped to allow for the business of horses and carriages. However, a consistent level of architectural control extends on beyond the stable block to include outbuildings, boundary walls and the curved wall with gates to the forecourt that is joined to the south wing of the Provost's House. In this way the elaborately decorated architecture of the outer screen surrounds and encloses an everyday working environment, the stable yard itself.

To a certain extent the larger project of the boundary wall and railings to the College, starting from the eastern end of Nassau Street in 1842 and eventually encompassing the Provost's House Stables site, had the effect of swamping some of the strategic presence of Darley's design. Encircled though it is by its sweep of the railings' continuity, the architectural intentions of his quietly insistent granite statement remain legible through the veiling layer of Mallet's cast iron masterwork.

Little has changed within the setting of this sheltered courtyard since its completion in 1844. The stable went out of use for horses in the 1930s and since then had been vacant or used for storage purposes. In the changeover from horse to car, the coach house was partitioned as a garage and its archway and some of the windows blocked up. Despite some years of genteel neglect, the structure and fabric of the building survived substantially intact.

When we first visited the site in April 2005, we noted the inwardness and austerity of the stable yard. Within the building, the difference in function and character between the two levels was clearly legible in their respective flooring materials. Upstairs, haylofts and rooms for grooms and coachmen had unvarnished timber floor boarding throughout. Downstairs, a granite flagstone floor ran through the

Fig. 2 – Cross section showing Reading Room over study carrels. Courtesy O'Donnell+Tuomey.

Fig. 3 – Granite floor of classroom with view to stable yard, and doorway to study carrels.
Photo, Ros Kavanagh.

rooms, with areas of brick flooring local to the horse stalls. Gulleys carved in the granite provided rills for run-off from the loose boxes and stalls to drains in the cobbled yard. The building was dark with solid doors and louvred screens to the hay lofts. One double-hinged door folded back flat against the wall when fully opened; its two-part action provided extra width for manoeuvring horses in and out. These signs of use, and other distinctive details and characteristics of the existing building, were surveyed and recorded as evidence for further reference in the detailed specifications of the refurbishment and repairs.

The rooms in the existing building were dark because of the small windows and the provision of windows on the north facing elevation only. Our design challenge was to look for ways to improve daylight to the rooms without compromising the one-way facing character of the building.

Analysis of the composition of the north elevation revealed three areas of fenestration grouped around three vertical axes. In order to increase the daylight to the upper floor reading room and offices, we moved the circulation to the rear, opened up the single blind window and fully glazed two existing hayloft door openings. These three openings formed the basis of the rhythm of the original elevational design. One of the original sash windows had been replaced by an open louvre screen for ventilation of the hayloft. Given the requirement to maintain privacy to the Provost's garden, the precedent of the existing timber louvres was adapted to the design of the newly glazed openings. The central doorway to the

Fig. 4 – North elevation analysis.
Courtesy O'Donnell+Tuomey.

Opposite: *Fig. 5* – Study carrels in the horse stalls.
Photo, Ros Kavanagh.

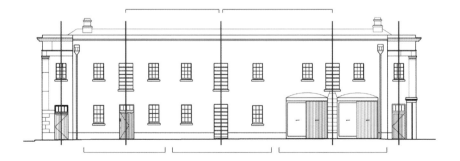

Fig. 6 – The carriage room opened up.
Photo, Ros Kavanagh.

Fig. 7 – New into old. Photo, Ros Kavanagh.

ground floor stalls was opened up in the same manner, to provide daylight for research students' carrels.

Giving equal expression to three upper, and one lower, floor openings unified the elevational composition consistent with the original design. In order to admit daylight to the classroom in the former carriage room, we glazed one-half of each existing under-arch opening and re-hung the two surviving doors as external sliding shutters. Timber-boarded screen walling, behind each sliding shutter in its open position, allows for control of daylight to provide the blackout conditions required for presentations in the classroom. The north elevation had been resurfaced in cement plaster. This inappropriate material was removed and a stone pigmented lime render was reinstalled.

Jane Smiley (a novelist who has written extensively about horses), in her book *13 Ways of Looking at the Novel*,[1] describes the experience of the process of exchange between writer and reader and how the book, once read, belongs to both: 'Something in one form in the mind takes another form on the page; something in one form on the page takes another form in the mind'. Elsewhere, Anne Michaels, author of *Fugitive Pieces*, further analyses the role of the translator: 'The poet moves from life to language, the translator moves from language to life; both try to identify the invisible, what's between the lines, the mysterious implications.'[2]

It is the author's effort to put life into language; the translator's role is to find the life within that language. Working on conversion projects such as this, where the setting and theme of the architecture have been so clearly established by another architect in another time, the incoming architect forsakes his usual role as author/designer to become a reader/translator of the given material. We took all our decisions on this project in this spirit: the position of a redundant chimney shaft gave us the location for the introduction of the required vertical services; the array of five stalls with their timber screens showing scratchmarks from years of use provided the requisite fifteen study bays for researchers. Close reading and sensitive translation should prevent the unwitting introduction of extraneous elements or inappropriate interventions that inadvertently undermine the setting. This is not merely a precautionary measure to reduce risk of damage to original material. There is pleasure to be drawn from this reading and translation. Research allows opportunities for clear observation. Measured survey provides a satisfying basis for semi-surgical procedures.

The particular qualities of the Stable building, the physical materials and sensory character residual from its former use, engender a different response from us in our time than would have been registered as of any unusual significance at the time of construction. In Darley's day, granite flagstones, brick floors, lime pigments and plasters would have been basic building materials, pure and simple. They remain so today, but such economy of means takes on an element of luxury when re-presented in a transformed context. The brick floors act like carpets in the concentrated study areas; the rough granite slabs connect the circulation spaces with the specific atmosphere of the cobbled yard.

[1]   Jane Smiley, *13 Ways of Looking at the Novel* (London, 2006), p. 84.

[2]   Anne Michaels, *Fugitive Pieces* (London, 1997), p. 109.

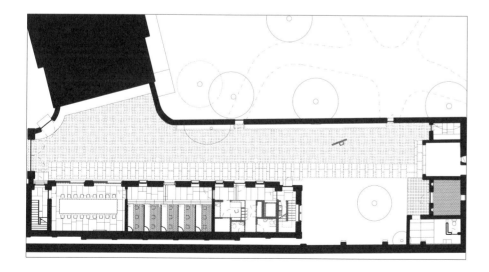

Fig. 8 – Ground floor plan after conversion. Courtesy O'Donnell+Tuomey

STABLES AND HORSES IN IRELAND *c.* 1630–1840

Patricia McCarthy

INTRODUCTION

Every man in the British Dominions that knows me knows, as Well as I do, that my Sole Amusement is my Horses, and that I neither play Cards or Dice, keep neither Whores nor Hounds[1]

So wrote Sir Edward O'Brien (1705–65) of Dromoland to his son, Lucius, in response to his heir's plea to sell some of his horses to pay debts in 1758. The inscription over the entrance to the grand quadrangular stables built in 1736 by Sir Edward, *In Equus Patrum Virius* (the strength of a nation is in its horses), leaves one in no doubt of his pride in them and his care in their accommodation. One hundred years earlier, Roger Boyle, the 1st Earl of Orrery (1621–79) would have concurred with this proud statement. He was eulogised for 'His care to breed brave horses thou would'st ride/In peace for pleasure and in war for fight'.[2] While the two men would have shared the enjoyment and the challenges of breeding horses, it was part of Orrery's job, as Cromwell's Master of the Ordnance in Ireland, to provide horses for war. The attitudes of these men to the horses under their care are indicative of the circumstances that led to the development of stable architecture in Ireland, the subject of this essay.

The building of stables in country and town in Ireland will be examined over a period of just over two hundred years up to the 1840s, when Frederick Darley's stables for the Provost's House were built. It will endeavour to put together, from sources such as surviving buildings, architectural plans and excerpts from letters, what little knowledge there is about stable architecture during that time. In order to put the stables into a context, it is necessary to appreciate and discuss the many roles played by the horse during this period. The essay does not pretend to be an in-depth study of either stables or horses, but will look at both under three headings relating to the functions of horses: military, pleasure, and transport. In the section on the military, the various stables built over the years at Dublin Castle are examined, as is the building of those at the Royal (now Collins) Barracks. Dublin

Castle was the centre of power in the country, the official residence of the viceroy, and a military centre in which barracks and stables were located. The design and state of the Castle's stables might be a yardstick by which a visitor would judge others. The Royal Barracks, the 'largest and most complete barracks in Europe'[3] was the first residential barracks built in an urban location in Ireland and Britain. There, and at the Castle, riding houses were built where the ancient art of horsemanship was practised, with the aid of Lord Molesworth's book of rules.[4] The pleasures of the horse include hunting and racing and the building of private stables. The third section, on the rather mundane but essential aspect of transport, will include carriages and their equipage in their twin roles of travel and display, and will focus on stables or mews buildings.

MILITARY

Immediately upon his arrival in Dublin as Lord Deputy in July 1633, Thomas Wentworth, later 1st Earl of Strafford (1593–1641), began building a new stable at Dublin Castle to accommodate thirty-six horses for his bodyguard.[5] This was possibly the first major stable project to be undertaken in this country. Three months later, in a letter to one of the Secretaries of State, he stated that the horse was to play a more prominent role in the passage of the Lord Deputy through the streets. He added that a church which had heretofore been used as the Castle stable would revert to its former use, and that the stable being built would be ready by June 1634.[6] Wentworth, a man who was keenly aware of the propaganda possibilities of architecture (as well as of fine horses) and who fancied himself as an architect, designed the building, as he boasts in a letter to Lord Arundel. The letter, incidentally, shows that he felt himself in competition with Inigo Jones, the Surveyor of the King's Works:

> *I desire peace with ye great and good genius of Architecture Mr Inigoe Jones, Soe*
> *as it may be wthout negelect to us ye lesser Intelligences in yt [that] high and*

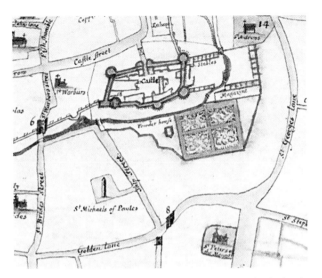

Fig. 1 – Bernard de Gomme, *The Citty and Suburbs of Dublin* (1673). Detail showing the location of the stables at Dublin Castle and the River Poddle, which flows across the stable yard. © National Maritime Museum, London.

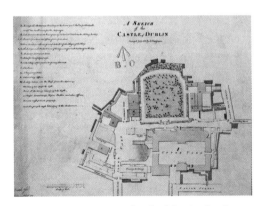

Fig. 2 – H. Chaigneau, A Sketch of the Castle of Dublin (1801) showing the stable yard and the riding house. The National Archives, London, MPH1/202(1).

noble art… But if he look big and distainfully upon us, I shall not forbear to tell him, I have built a better stable for ye King here in Ireland than ever he did in England.[7]

Major General Sir William Brereton, who visited the Castle in 1635, supported that view, declaring it a 'gallant, stately stable, as any I have seen in the King's dominions' that had been 'lately erected'.[8] An account written thirty-eight years later by another visitor to the Castle refers to the same stables. With the help of two documents created that year, 1673, it is possible to pinpoint exactly where they were located. The first is a plan of the Castle[9] where a 'Posterne Gate' is shown to the north-east of the complex, south of the Powder Tower. It was through here that the visitor, Robert Ware, was admitted and from where he

descend[ed]… into the Stable Yard… there may you behold large statelie stables of an elegant contrivance build in ye time of ye Earl of Strafford… there passeth through the Stable yard a full stream of water, issueing out the Castle gardens which plentifully serves to all uses belonging unto the horse there kept, and to the several artificers….[10]

The gate can be just about made out on Bernard de Gomme's map of Dublin (1673, fig. 1), on which the location of the stables is clearly marked,[11] on the north side of the Lower Yard, the site of the present Treasury block. Measuring 142 feet by 50 feet, the 'Grand Stables' as they appear on a survey map of 1684, accommodated only thirty horses, and the River Poddle, the 'full stream of water', that looks rather more substantial than a mere stream on de Gomme's map, is called a 'Horse Pond'[12] in the later plan.[13] Brereton describes the building as

a double stable, there being a strong wall in the middle, to either side whereof stand the horses' heads. Thirty horses may stand at ease on either side, the stalls being very large; these are exceeding high, at least five or six yards, and very near the same breadth…

By the time that John Dunton saw these stables some years later, in 1697, they had perhaps lost their 'stateliness', as his description of them as 'not extraordinary… but convenient and big enough' is rather low-key.[14] By 1714, according to Edward McParland, 'one range of Burgh's new stables' was built. As it cannot have been on

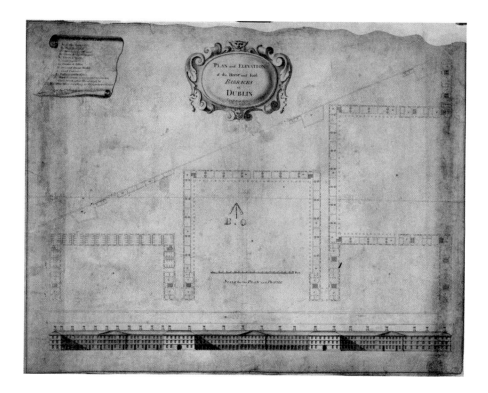

Fig. 3 – James Bastide, Dublin Barracks (1722). Copy after Burgh's elevation and plan. Horse Square (later Cavalry Square) is located to the left. The National Archives, London, MPH 1/592.

the site of the old stables because the Treasury building was begun there at about that time,[15] it is likely that they were moved closer to the riding house below the Lower Yard (fig. 2).

In 1703 the Lord Lieutenant, the 2nd Duke of Ormonde, recommended the building of a barracks in Dublin and a plan was drawn up by Thomas Burgh (1670–1730), the Engineer and Surveyor General, for the Royal Barracks.[16] Part of this large complex was to house cavalry, and the stables in Horse Square (later Cavalry Square), located on each of the three sides, were fitted out for approximately 150 horses, each stall corresponding with the troopers' quarters above.[17] According to James Douet, the layout of the stables was typical of eighteenth-century cavalry barracks, with five stalls either side of a passage leading from front to back, different in plan to Wentworth's design (fig. 3).[18]

Fig. 4 – Illustration from William Cavendish, Duke of Newcastle, *Méthode et invention nouvelle…* (London, 1737 edn.).

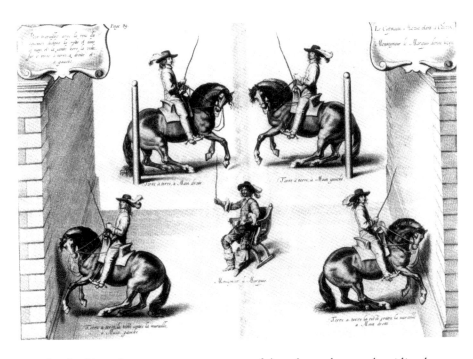

Another building that was a necessary part of these barracks was the riding house. Giles Worsley defines this type of building as 'a covered, barn-like structure'.[19] In it the art of horsemanship was learned and refined, aimed primarily at the military for whom obedience and manoeuvrability in their horses, particularly on a battlefield, were obviously important. An ancient art form, it was practised by noblemen at courts in England and elsewhere in Europe from the time of Henry VIII.[20] In the second half of the sixteenth century there was a growing and necessary interest in the breeding of horses in England not just for war, which was the primary reason, but also for the challenge and enjoyment of being able to produce a well-trained horse (fig. 4).[21] From the early sixteenth century numerous books on horsemanship were published, probably the most influential being that published in 1667 by William Cavendish, Duke of Newcastle, who, at about the same time, built a riding school at his castle at Bolsover, Derbyshire. The political atmosphere in Ireland during these years precluded gentlemen in this country from the joys of such activities unless they were in the military.

Thomas Burgh in 1705/6 received a part-payment of £200 for building 'a Riding Hous [*sic*] in the Castle Yard' at Dublin Castle, and a payment of £25 (on a quarterly basis) was made to 'Lieut Noah Regnaut Masr of the Rideing House'.[22] This is the 'Riding House' seen on John Rocque's 1756 map of Dublin, next to a stable yard.[23] It is possible that this building replaced an earlier one, as indicated by Ware's comment in 1673 about the stable yard at the Castle 'where you may take delight in seeing the great horse ridden and managed by the rules of the best horsemanship, and of martiall skill…'.[24] At the Royal Barracks in 1746 Arthur Jones Nevill (Surveyor General 1743–52) began a chapel to serve the military community that was converted almost immediately into a riding school. This led to an anonymous single-sheet publication mocking Nevill: 'He also built the new Beautifull Grand Chapple to the *B—-ks* of *D-bl-n*, where his art of pitching a Roof is fully displayed… but as a Monument of his great Skill, it is now converted into a Riding-house…'.[25] This too can be seen on Rocque's map, a rectangular block directly behind Royal Square. The riding house was where, according to the book of rules written by Lord Molesworth in 1744 (revised 1745), new or 'aukward' horses were brought each morning to be trained 'by gentle Degrees, so as never to disgust a young Horse, by being too rough with him'. New recruits, in groups of twelve moving in a circle around the riding master, were taught to mount and dismount properly, to sit well in their saddles and to ensure that 'their legs, bridle-hands and sword-hands be well placed'.[26]

While no information has come to light about the appearance of the riding house at the Castle, that for the Royal Barracks has survived, recently refurbished and now used as an exhibition space by the National Museum.[27] Built of rubble-stone, it is four bays deep; the west front of the riding house is a gable of three bays with a central round-topped doorway over which is an oculus, and two round-topped windows are placed at a high level and towards the sides of the front. The windows and oculus are surrounded in brick while the door has a stone surround. With a roof span of 59 feet (18m) it was a remarkable example of eighteenth-century roof technology.[28]

It is fair to say that in Ireland there would have been few riding houses on private demesnes (for the training of the owner's horses) at any time, though one was being built at Curraghmore, County Waterford, in 1835.[29] Worsley says that only a few are known to have been built in the British Isles in the period between 1660 and 1740; he refers to that at Dublin Castle as for the use of the Lord Lieutenant, the Duke of Ormonde, 'who kept his own quasi-royal court'.[30] However, stable-building was another matter and some of the earliest references to owners of stables apply to the Ormonde family.

PLEASURE

In addition to his remarks about the stables at Dublin Castle on his tour in Ireland in 1635, Brereton noted those attached to Ormond Castle in Carrick-on-Suir, belonging to the Earl (later Duke) of Ormond, another soldier. Built *c.*1570 by Thomas Butler, the 10th Earl, the large stable block and yards were located to the north-west of the castle.[31] Brereton describes the location:

> *Here is my Lord of Ormond's house, daintily seated on the river bank, which flows even to the walls of his house, which I went to see, and found in the outer court three or four haystacks, not far from the stable door; this court is paved.*[32]

There are references, too, to Ormond's stables at Kilkenny Castle in a survey of 1654–6 which describes the 'Great Stable' as 'a double building divided into 2 parts 96 x 38'.[33] It is possible that this might be the double block shown in Rocque's map of 1758. It would appear to be either here or at Carrick-on-Suir in 1662 that he considered replacing the stables with new ones resembling a royal hunting lodge in England, an indication of the importance that was attaching to stable building at that time.[34]

In April 1668, during his term as Lord Lieutenant, Ormonde was concerned to hear of an outbreak of disease at his stables in Carrick 'where the hopefullest colts and fillys are'.[35] It might be assumed that the aspiration for his horses was for both service to the Crown and for hunting. From the 1530s in England horse-breeding became subject to public policy, and it was during that century that the care taken to record the history of individual horses led to the keeping of pedigrees.[36] In Ireland after the Restoration, many gentlemen took horse-breeding very seriously: Colonel Daniel O'Brien from County Limerick wrote in 1670, 'I begin to be the greatest breeder of horses in the King's dominions, for I keep about my house 16,000 acres for my mares, colts and deer'.[37] Horses crossed the Irish Sea in both directions in order to improve strains; in 1685 it was estimated that 1,054 horses were exported to England. These included the Irish hobby, highly valued in England for short journeys.[38] In 1687 Lord Ossory paid the large sum of £129 for a horse, at a time when the average price of an ordinary horse was between five shillings and one pound.[39]

Horses were sometimes used by the aristocracy in the exchange of gifts: Lord Cork presented horses bred by him to both the King and the Duke of York in the 1660s. Service by a stallion was similarly in the gift of owners, an honour that could be bestowed on the mares of both peers and dependants, a form of altruism in itself.[40] In his will, Henry O'Brien, son of the 7th Earl of Thomond, left to his father 'any horse, mare, or gelding he chooses out of the stable'; knowing his father would choose his best horse, he willed to his 'dear friend' the 'next best horse' and so on.[41] The expense of breeding meant that it was unlikely to make an owner rich, but it had the power to strengthen social and political alliances.

While the stables were important to owners, the horse was their real concern and indeed, passion, sometimes to the exclusion of all else, with the possible exception of drinking.[42] Edward Pakenham described his friend Lord Buttevant in 1737 as 'a man the world may call a good natured man but... his abilities range little further than a pack of hounds or horses'.[43] But this passion had the potential to create tension in a family: Toby Barnard cites the inventory of goods left by Sir Philip Perceval in 1680 – pathetically few, but he had more than fifty horses in his stables, and work had begun on new kennels.[44] Lady Broghill complained of being 'eaten out of house and home, for my lord's horses, dogs and strange company do devour most unconscionable'.[45] Reference to the 'strange company' may have had a resonance almost a hundred years later when the Duchess of Northumberland wrote in her diary:

> *Men that are fond of Horses generally prefer the Stable to good Company &*
> *occupied with the Conversation of Jockeys Coachmen Grooms & postillions they*
> *contract in such Company a rude coarse manner of speaking wch destroys that*
> *politeness so necessary in the Society of Ladys by wch means they come to neglect*

them & often become swearers & Brutes. And the Ladys in return always reckon them to have little wit & much ignorance.[46]

THE STABLE OF THE PRIVATE HOUSE

Up to the first decades of the eighteenth century, descriptions of stable architecture in Ireland are even more rare than those for houses, but it might be possible to put a little flesh on the stables at Portmore, County Antrim, built by Lord Conway in 1671 close to his new castle, for which there are some details and the name of an architect. They were of two storeys, provided accommodation for two troop of horse,[47] and measured 140 feet long, 35 feet wide and 40 feet high.[48] According to Rolf Loeber, Conway sent from England to his agent in Ireland drawings for these by William Hurlbutt, together with drawings of stables at Cornbury Park, Oxfordshire[49] which were deemed to be a good model. Conway approved of Hurlbutt's designs but, as a military man, he was unhappy with the plan: 'I dislike the Ovall Figure and have altered it to Sex Angular as the more defensible…'.[50] That the plans were sophisticated there can be no doubt when we look at William or Roger Hurlbutt's surviving stable at Tredegar House, Gwent (before 1680, fig. 5), and a description of that at Warwick Castle (1667). In both cases Ionic pilasters on the exterior stop short of the cornice, and are interspersed with *oeil-de-boeuf* windows. Worsley argues persuasively that the pilasters announce the purpose of the building on its exterior: within contemporary stables the heelposts of the stalls were frequently in the Doric or Ionic orders, topped with a ball or an acorn. This would account for the pineapple motif on the pilasters at Tredegar. There, too, the design of the block paralleled that of the house, and bore similarities to the stable block at Cornbury, with a pedimented centrepiece and projecting wings.[51] Portmore, too, had projecting wings, but whether Hurlbutt's overall plan was built is unknown and the stables were demolished in 1763.[52]

An early plan by Thomas Smith of Burton House, County Cork (1671), shows a layout that bridged the transition between the early seventeenth-century fortified castles and later unfortified houses: two enclosures (with turrets on each

Fig. 5 – Tredegar House, Gwent, exterior of stables (c. 1670). ©2008 William Curtis Rolf. All rights reserved.

corner in case of attack) are surrounded by curtain walls: one contains the pleasure garden to the rear, and the other contains the house with its various courts, farm buildings and stables. The stables measured 60 feet by 20 feet and included two coachhouses (fig. 6).[53]

By the end of the seventeenth century, stables were becoming important status symbols in Ireland among the nobility and gentry, somewhere to take one's guests to view, not just the building, but also the horses within it. As with works of art, the appreciation of horses also required a deal of connoisseurship. There was a difference, too, between stables that accommodated farm horses and those that accommodated riding and carriage horses, racehorses and hunters, the latter ranges located closer to the house and usually of some architectural interest. No longer would the seventeenth-century verses in which a dwelling was mistaken for a stable apply:

> *Ned he alights and leads (god bless us all)*
> *His horse into his worship's very hall;*
> *And looking round about, cries in great anger,*
> *'zowns, here's a stable, has no rack nor manger.'*
> *'Peace Ned', (quoth I) 'prithe be no so gasty;*
> *This room's no stable though it be nasty;*
> *I see a harp and chimney too, and dare*
> *Say there was a fire in't before the war;*
> *So this is no place for a horse you see.'*
> *'Tis then for very beast, I'm sure', quotes he.*[54]

Thomas Dineley, on his tour of Ireland (and France) 1675–80, describes the stable at Rallahine, County Clare, with its dormers and doorway with scrolled pediment, as the 'fairest stable of the countrye'.[55] Stables became separate from the farm buildings, built of more expensive materials both inside and out. But the real change came in the first decades of the eighteenth century, when Edward Lovett Pearce provided plans, and possibly supervised building, at Castletown House (built 1722–5) in County Kildare.

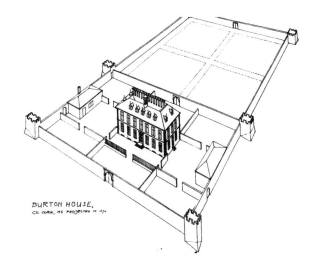

BURTON HOUSE,
CO. CORK, AS PROJECTED IN 17-

Fig. 6 – Rolf Loeber, Reconstruction drawing of Burton House, County Cork (1972), with permission.

Pearce may well have provided drawings for Castletown before his grand tour, during which he spent much time in Vicenza studying the buildings of Andrea Palladio. He was responsible for the introduction of Palladianism to Ireland, a style that changed the face of domestic building in the country and the architectural taste of not only the aristocracy, but also the gentry. Castletown, the first example in Ireland of a Palladian layout – a central block linked by colonnaded quadrants to pavilions that accommodated the kitchen in one, and the stables in the other – began a trend in country house design that was continued by Richard Castle, his assistant, well after Pearce's early death in 1733. It is interesting that Ireland differed from Britain where the pavilions were generally not used for stables, but for apartments and offices: Worsley has pointed out that, just as neo-Palladianism became the dominant architectural style, most iconic Palladian houses in England, such as Wanstead in Essex, appeared isolated in the landscape, with stables placed to one side.[56] This occurred much later in Ireland, as shall be seen.

Pearce's proposal to give the stable pavilion at Stillorgan House, Dublin, a face-lift with Diocletian windows set in blank arcading was the standard neo-Palladian formula for stable buildings in Britain devised by William Kent and Lord Burlington.[57] His seven-bay stable pavilion at Castletown is vaulted, supported by Tuscan columns that act as heelposts for the stalls. Vaulting became one of the features of Castle's stable architecture, used at Carton and other houses[58] (fig. 7) and, though common in Ireland, it was exceptional even in aristocratic stables in Britain, where it was considered to be too expensive for most owners (fig. 8).[59]

In Ireland there were owners who were willing to spend much money and time on their horses, as has been seen. The O'Briens at Dromoland, County Clare, were as famous for their stable as they were for gambling. Lady O'Brien's horse was painted with her saddle of blue velvet trimmed with silver, the O'Brien racing colours (fig. 9). The inscription over the entrance to the stable quadrangle built in 1736 by Sir Edward O'Brien announces its importance.[60] The Dromoland Album[61] contains a number of drawings for stable buildings, one of which shows a nine-bay single storey building where the projecting central three bays bear a pediment within which is an *oeil-de-boeuf* window, another motif which was popular in stable buildings, having the practical advantage of providing light and air in the hayloft.[62] Another shows a quadrangular stable layout with the buildings in the Palladian style, featuring central rusticated and

Fig. 8 – Richard Castle, Vaulted stable at Strokestown House, County Roscommon. Photo, the author.

Opposite: *Fig. 7* – George Nairn ARHA (1799–1850), *The interior of the stables at Carton, County Kildare; a liveried groom, Lord Charles William FitzGerald and his sister Lady Jane Seymour FitzGerald.* Oil on canvas, *c.* 1825. Photo courtesy Mallett & Son (Antiques) Ltd., London and New York.

Fig. 9 – James Seymour (attrib.), *Lady O'Brien's horse with a running footman* (1740s) showing the O'Brien racing colours of blue and silver. Private collection.

Fig. 10 – John Aheron (attrib.), Elevation of stable block in the Palladian style. The Dromoland Album, NLI MS 2791. Photo courtesy Irish Architectural Archive.

pedimented loggia fronts, niches and sunken panels containing husk chains; and others have cupolas with clocks and finials over arched and pedimented carriageways (figs. 10 and 11). According to Worsley, the quadrangular stable layout was rare in Britain before the eighteenth century, except for the monarchy, although a plan for one appeared in Colen Campbell's *Vitruvius Britannicus* (1725) for Houghton Hall, Norfolk. Eschewing the neo-Palladian idea of incorporating stables in the wings of houses in favour of a detached quadrangular block standing proudly in the landscape,[63] it began a trend in Britain, but not yet in Ireland, despite Sir Edward's example.

By the mid-eighteenth century, the Palladian plan was well established in Ireland and can be seen in Richard Castle's (unexecuted) plan for Castlecoole, County Fermanagh, where two stable yards, located behind curved curtain walls to the east and west, have accommodation for thirty-six horses and five coaches (fig. 12). The proximity of the stable yard to the house was something that Frances Power Cobbe at Newbridge House, County Dublin, enjoyed as a child, when her nursery had three

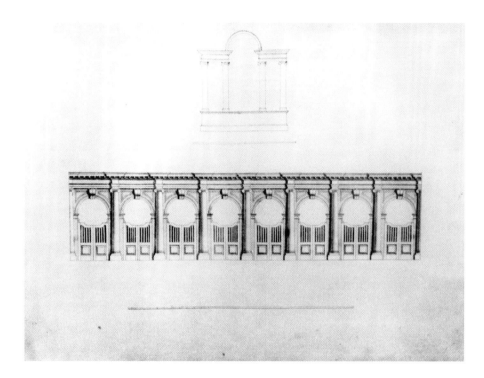

Fig. 11 – John Aheron (attrib.), Classical eight-bay elevation for stable stalls in the Ionic order with engaged columns, entablature and a robust scrolled keystone. The Dromoland Album, NLI MS 2791. Photo courtesy Irish Architectural Archive.

windows overlooking it to the east of the house.[64] A rather late (1789) Palladian design by James Byres for Charleville Forest, County Offaly, shows an entrance cut across the quadrant passage, where the occupants of a coach could be deposited under cover, before it continued into the stable yard. By this time, the Palladian style had run its course, and the stable block or the quadrangular stables, built at a short distance from the house, were the preferred options for owners. Before looking at some of these, a brief look at the interior of stables might be of interest.

Stables for horses used by the family for their own use (riding, hunting, racing and carriages), and located closest to the house, generally accommodated between fourteen and twenty-eight horses. Castle's plans at both Castlecoole and Headfort, County Meath, indicate differences in stable fittings: at Headfort one stable accommodates '6 Horses in Stalls' and the other '8 Horses in Bails', and at Castlecoole one is for '4 Horses in Stalls' while the other, of the same dimensions, is annotated 'Common stable for 6 Horses'. The merits or otherwise of 'bails', or the

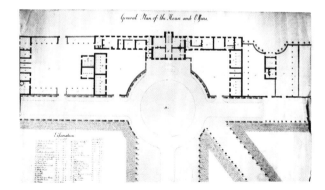

Fig. 12 – Richard Castle, Unexecuted plan of house and offices for Castlecoole, County Fermanagh (undated). Reproduced with the permission of Lord Belmore. Photo courtesy Irish Architectural Archive.

hanging bale (a partition comprising a wooden bar hanging horizontally on a chain or a leather thong between the manger and the heelpost)(fig. 13), versus the stall (a fixed partition), were debated in England in the late sixteenth century and early seventeenth century.[65] While the Irish and the French continued the use of the bale well into the eighteenth century, it had 'fallen out of favour in the better class of British stable' by the beginning of the century.[66] The bale was approved by Roger North, 'for the horses doe not love to be recluse, but hanker after the enjoyment of their company, which is by the eye, so have pleasing converse', and recommended a post and partition at the manger as it 'prevents snapping, and unequall feeding… if they can come at each other's meat'. He allowed a space within the stable of five feet to each horse. [67]

Writers were at one in their advice for stables: all stressed the need for plenty of air (preferably a current of air running through the building), light and good drainage.[68] Flooring was important: wooden planks were common into the seventeenth century, as were cobbles. While planks were dangerously slippery, cobbles were difficult to clean and could present an uneven surface for the horse.[69] Bricks, or clinkers, were used in Lord Strafford's stable at Dublin Castle, a point made by Brereton on his 1635 visit: 'no planks [are] made use of, but Holland bricks placed upon edges, whereon the horses lie and you walk; these as easy to walk upon as to lie upon, and these are made of Holland earth, which is harder and more durable than our clay'.[70]

There are some interesting designs from the second half of the eighteenth century, when stables became architectural entities in their own right, built in a variety of styles. A vast forecourt that is quite unique in Ireland was provided by the architect John Roberts for the Earl of Tyrone at Curraghmore, County Waterford, and built between 1750 and 1760. Thirty-one bay, two-storey stable ranges on each side of the tree-lined forecourt[71] are punctuated by monumental pedimented archways with blocked columns and pilasters that give access to the stable yards (fig. 14). The early nineteenth-century stable buildings attached to two houses in County Limerick, Stoneville and Glenville, both belonging to branches of the Massy family (one of the great hunting families in Ireland), might confirm the oft-quoted remark that stable buildings in Ireland were often better than the houses to which they were attached. Others of note include Lancelot 'Capability' Brown's Gothic quadrangular stables at Slane Castle, County Meath (prior to 1783), and the stable and farm office ranges by Robert Adam at Castle Upton, County Antrim (1788), that include towers, turrets and pyramidal roofed pavilions (for coaches), described by Mark Bence-Jones as 'the most important surviving range of office buildings in Adam's castle style'.[72] The difference in materials used in stable and farm yards is visible at Carriglas, County Longford (1794–6), where James Gandon's square stable yard, entered through a handsome pedimented archway, is of a blue-grey limestone ashlar, while the farmyard is rendered with stone dressings.

In the early nineteenth century the 2nd Earl of Belmore commissioned Richard Morrison to design a stable court and offices for Castlecoole, for which a number of drawings survive (figs. 15 and 16).[73] An interesting quadrangular plan and section (unexecuted) allows fourteen stalls each for coach horses, saddle horses and

Fig. 14 – Gateway to stable yard at Curraghmore, County Waterford. Photo, David Griffin. Courtesy Irish Architectural Archive.

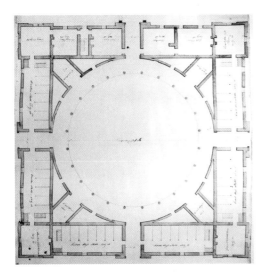

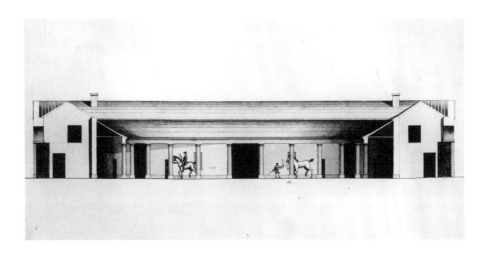

Figs. 15 & 16 – Richard Morrison, plan of stables and section illustrating horses being exercised in the circular colonnade. Reproduced with the permission of Lord Belmore. Photo courtesy Irish Architectural Archive.

Fig. 17 – Covered ride or 'Riding School' at Russborough House, County Wicklow. Photo, the author.

hunters: within the court is a circular colonnaded and covered riding area. Covered rides (open to one side) were known in England from the mid-1780s and were often used to exercise sickly horses, or in the event of bad weather (fig. 17).[74] The stables and offices as built at Castlecoole were tucked away, accessible by an underground tunnel from the basement of the house,[75] allowing the house its unfettered isolation. So, too, at Ballyfin, County Laois, where, with the aid of strategically placed planting, neither was visible from the approach to the house. At about the same time as Frederick Darley drew up plans for the Provost's House Stables at Trinity College, Richard Morrison designed a new façade for the offices and stables at Howth Castle, County Dublin (*c.* 1840), in an eclectic mix of styles: a Gothic entrance front on the north, crenellations and cruciform arrow slits on the east, and a circular tower at the north-east angle.[76] There the ubiquitous cupola and clock were to be found. The cupola was, as Worsley states, 'one of the most familiar images of the Georgian country house':[77] that at Ballyfin's eighteenth-century stables surmounted a pedimented breakfront on the north range and it bore a clock,[78] an item that was considered essential in the stable yard (fig. 18).[79]

The vast amounts of money expended by owners on stable designs by some of the top architects of the time underlines the lengths to which they went to ensure the well-being of their horses and the approbation of their peers. Through their sporting pursuits they could enjoy both equally.

HUNTING

Their nobility are much given to recreations and pastimes as hunting, hawking, riding, drinking, feasting and banqueting with one another....[80]

Hunting with hounds became well established in Ireland during the course of the sixteenth and seventeenth centuries, when the quarry included deer, hare, wild boar and wolves (fig.19). A mid-seventeenth-century poem in Irish describes the hunting conditions of the time and how, when the day's hunting was over, the family harper entertained the assembled sportsmen as they ate.[81] Phoenix Park in Dublin was originally a deer park laid out as a hunting ground for the viceroy. A visitor to Ireland in 1698, John Dunton, described hunting in Connemara with eighteen footmen and eighteen 'long greyhounds' which yielded a number of stags.[82] Foxes were regarded as vermin, and became a popular prey during the seventeenth century.[83] One of the earliest and best-known paintings of a foxhunt is *The Killruddery Hunt*, dating to *c.* 1740, on which the hounds, huntsmen, horses and stags are cut-outs that have

Fig. 18 – William Ashford, *The Stables at Mount Merrion House, County Dublin* (c. 1806). Fitzwilliam Museum, Cambridge.

Fig. 19 – Robert Richard Scanlan, *Hunting scene* (from a set of five), watercolour. Photo courtesy The Gorry Gallery, Dublin.

been stuck onto the surface of the picture (fig. 20).[84] A writer in 1719 observed of the Irish: 'The Ponsonby family at Bishopscourt, County Kildare kept a substantial racing establishment, where the frenetic pace of the hunting fraternity is illustrated in a letter written by a guest at that house to his wife in 1726 describing his day's activities: "… I went to bed last night at one of ye clock, was on horseback this morning at four, rid eight miles before daybreak, hunted a fox afterwards, came back afterwards here to dinner, and rid a coursing this afternoon till nightfall, and I thank God I cannot say I am much the worse for it" '.[85] Another example of the commitment to the chase was an account of the Earl of Meath's heir, who managed to hunt in Kildare during the season while staying at the family seat at Killruddery, County Wicklow in the 1820s:

> [He kept] his hunters in County Kildare, and having two hacks, one in Dublin and one at Kilruddery, riding into town, changing there, & going to wherever the meet took place, where his hunter awaited him. The return journey made in the same way and a hard gallop the entire distance. On one occasion they killed near the Hill of Allen, n.e. of the Curragh, and he returned that night in time for dinner as my Grandparents were very particular about punctuality.[86]

But it was not just the men who had such stamina. Lady Hester Westenra kept her own pack of hounds in County Laois and managed to strike a bargain for her purse

when approached by a highwayman during a hunt in the 1740s. Together they raced after the hounds which had just broken covert: after a long run which Hester won with ease, she offered him her purse but the highwayman bowed and graciously refused to take it.[87] Another enthusiast, Hayes St Leger, the 4th Viscount Doneraile, kept a hunting journal in which he kept an account of hunts in which he took part in both Ireland and England. He recorded the route taken, the numbers of hares and foxes killed and which horse he rode.[88] He probably should have known better than to keep a pet fox from which he caught rabies, resulting in his death in France where he had gone in search of a cure from Louis Pasteur.[89]

Tom Conolly, one of the founders of organised horse-breeding and racing in Ireland,[90] imported horses from the best studs in England to improve the breeds.[91]

Fig. 20 – Anonymous, *The Killruddery Hunt* (c.1740), oil on panel onto which cut-out riders and animals are applied. Photo, the author. Reproduced with the permission of Lord Meath.

He was also famous for his open-handed hospitality and those who hunted with him in Kildare were automatically invited to eat at Castletown, as the following verse describes:

> But the best-mounted man at that gay covert side
> Is honest Tom Conolly, Castletown's pride;
> All mirth and good fellowship beam in his eye
> Such a goodly collection of guests to descry.
> For guests shall be all
> In Tom Conolly's hall
> Who keeps open house for the great and the small,
> And none who takes share in the fox hunt to-day
> 'Ere midnight from Castletown's mansion shall stray.[92]

A series of studies painted by Robert Healy in February 1768 records the Conollys and their friends as they hunted and occupied themselves with other outdoor activities at Castletown (fig. 21).[93] As early as 1723 there was a pack of foxhounds in Balrath, County Meath,[94] and by mid-century numerous others appeared across the country. A pack of hounds was kept at Newbridge House, County Dublin, where, in the 1840s, various relations of the Cobbe family 'arrived by coachloads,

Fig. 21 – Robert Healy, Tom Conolly of Castletown hunting with his Friends, (1768). Pastel, chalk and gouache on paper. Yale Center for British Art, Paul Mellon Collection, USA.

with trains of servants, [where] they remained for months at a time' in order to hunt, play cards and to enjoy other activities.[95] Seventy to eighty hounds were kept at Eyrecourt, County Galway, that howled, it was said, whenever psalms were sung in the local church.[96] Tom Conolly from Castletown, who had a well-established pack by 1764, later imported foxhounds from the Duke of Rutland's famous pack at Belvoir Castle in England.[97] The excellence of hounds, as well as of horses, reflected well on the owner, so breeding was important, with strains imported from continental Europe as well as England to improve the breeds.[98] Hounds were also exchanged as gifts.

HUNTING LODGES

Keen hunting men who spent much of the winter months indulging in the sport sometimes built a hunting box or lodge with stables at a distance from their homes, where they could devote themselves entirely to the enjoyment of the chase and the post-chase entertainment.

In the early 1770s Louisa Conolly wrote to her husband from her family seat at Goodwood, encouraging him to acquire a hunting lodge there: 'it would be an additional expence, but still I think not more than you can well afford…'.[99] Her father, the Duke of Richmond, was the Master of the Charlton Hunt, the most

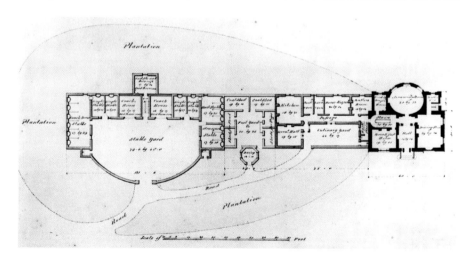

Fig. 22 – Richard Morrison, *Design for Hunting Lodge and Offices for the Earl of Belmore* (1768). Reproduced with the permission of Lord Belmore. Photo courtesy Irish Architectural Archive.

famous in England, and had built a hunting lodge in the village in 1732, as did other noblemen. A letter to Sir Thomas Taylor at Bective House, Smithfield, Dublin describes a visit to the Duke of Richmond's seat in 1742, after which the writer 'made a visit to a nest of fox hunters at Charlton among whom were three dukes, several lords and everyone has a little lodge in the village, and a noble large Publick room,[100] and they spend the hunting season there'.[101] That the *après*-hunt was as enjoyable as the sport itself is underlined by Jonah Barrington's description of the scene when he called to his brother's hunting lodge at Castle Durrow, County Laois, the morning after a dinner party. There he found:

> *the Baccanalians asleep, some upon chairs, the others on the floor. All candles were burned to the socket. Glasses, dishes, plates, knives, and spoons lay mixed in glorious confusion, while the ground was strewn with empty bottles and heaps of bones picked clean by the dogs.[102]*

Kildare town may have been the Charlton of Ireland from Lord Chief Baron Willes' description in 1761: 'I lay at Kildare… a very pretty town by means of the gentlemen belonging to the Kildare Hunt. Their number is 61 and most of [them] have built for themselves little pretty lodges in the town for the convenience of hunting'.[103] Presumably Willes is writing of the lodges that appear on a map of the Curragh dating from 1807 that belonged to Conolly, Denis Bowes Daly, the La Touche family and others.[104] Some houses, such as Fota, County Cork, were built originally as hunting lodges, then extended to become houses: Sir William Chambers designed a hunting lodge (unexecuted) for Lord Charlemont in 1768,[105] and among the Castlecoole drawings is one for a lodge with extensive offices (fig. 22).[106]

RACING

In what must have been one of the earliest races at the Curragh, County Kildare – the Newmarket of Ireland – Lord Cork in 1634 'backed Lord Digby's horse against one of the Earl of Ormond's and lost a new beaver hat to Mr Ferrers, one of the Lord Deputy's gentlemen'.[107] Over a century later, prizes for races there, and at the seventy-two racecourses recorded throughout the country, had not increased greatly in value compared to the beaver hat; they were usually money, silver ornaments or perhaps a velvet saddle or a length of damask.[108] In the 1670s Charles II, in an effort to improve bloodstock, endowed prizes for races at the Curragh but, while it stimulated competition among breeders of racehorses, it did little to strengthen the working horses.[109] A decade later, when races were run on a regular basis at the Curragh, 'Dublin emptied and the work of governing Ireland ceased'.[110] Numerous landowners sponsored prizes at race meetings in their locality, generosity that could perhaps be translated later into votes. Meetings frequently lasted for a week and incorporated hunts and, in the evenings, entertainments, such as balls and theatricals, to facilitate the ladies. They were social occasions for people of all classes, including servants. In 1759 the Countess of Kildare gave her servants permission to attend the races that were being held in a field 'near Lyon's [house]', while she and her sister Sarah remained at Carton to take care of two of her children.[111] Their brother-in-law, Tom Conolly, together with other owners, frequently rode their own horses in races at the Curragh and elsewhere. Louisa Conolly wrote proudly to her sister in 1768 that her husband 'won 7 times out of eight' at the Curragh,[112] a feat that was repeated on many occasions (fig. 23). Because race meetings allegedly led to drunkenness among the peasants, Lord Kenmare suppressed the races at Killarney and the publicans were compensated for the loss by an abatement in their rent.[113] In 1739, in an effort to counteract the violence that often attended these meetings, the Irish parliament banned all races for prizes of less than £20.[114]

It was said of Sir Edward O'Brien that he called his home village Newmarket-on-Fergus after the English racecourse.[115] He built (in 1774) the two-storey octagonal gazebo on a hill close to the entrance to Dromoland, from which he could watch his horses as they exercised and raced.[116] But his gambling and lavish expenditure on the sport had to be momentarily curtailed when, to pay debts, he was forced to offer for sale in 1742 his entire stud of 'Brood Mares, Colts and Fillies of all Ages', using the face-saving excuse that the 'Lands and Demesne of Dromoland have been found… to be too rich and fatening for breeding galoping horses'.[117] In 1758, in response to a plea by his son, Lucius, to sell some of his horses, he wrote: 'Every man in the British Dominions that knows me knows, as Well as I do, that my Sole Amusement is my Horses, and that I neither play Cards or Dice, keep neither

Fig. 23 – Anonymous, *Race on the Curragh*, oil on canvas. Private collection. Photo, Photographic Survey, Courtauld Institute of Art.

Whores nor Hounds'.[118] This was not much comfort to his son, who saw his inheritance dwindling into debt. While his horses might have been O'Brien's only amusement, Lord Antrim's stable of racehorses bred by him at Glenarm was described in 1752 as his 'Chief amusement'. His stables were built on a nearby hill, where he also created a racecourse.[119]

TRANSPORT

The use and necessity of horses extended a lot further than war, the pomp and ceremony at Dublin Castle and sporting pursuits. They were valued at all levels: as working farm animals they pulled carts, wagons and ploughs, they served as mill-horses, transported goods and, later in the eighteenth century they delivered post, and pulled barges along canals. They were the primary mode of transport for centuries; attached to coaches and carriages, they worked singly or in teams, and as hacks or saddle horses they enabled individuals to travel the length and breadth of the country.

Apart from these practical advantages, the carriage and its horse were major fashion accessories, used to fullest effect in town where one's place in society could be judged by one's equipage. Mrs Pendarves (later Mrs Delany), at a military review in Phoenix Park in 1731 remarked 'Nobody's equipage outlooked ours except my Lord Lieutenant's, but in every respect I must say Mrs Clayton's (her host) *outshines* her neighbours'.[120] Lady Portarlington put it rather well:

> *The principal amusement now in Dublin is parading in part of the Circular road which lies between the park and the sea. It is the great source of pleasure and gallantry. The Duchess of Rutland has her six ponies there every morning, Lady Antrim six more, and the other ladies as many as they can get for love or money.*[121]

Display extended even to funerals, when the attendance of a family's coach and horses, even with nobody inside, was considered a courtesy to the deceased: the crest and livery of the servants indicated ownership.

Both coaches and coach horses were expensive. The horses had to be of the right size and appearance: as Barnard says, 'number, colour and breeding all became indices of standing and income': blacks and bays were the most desirable colours, and the minimum number for making an impact was six.[122] Fine horses were appreciated and attracted much attention. Ensuring that his new countess and her relatives would be impressed with the figure he cut, Lord Aldborough instructed his agent at Belan, County Kildare, to have 'a small corps of Light Horse' along with other military to escort the party as they approached his demesne. He also wanted 'two or four more black Coach horses to match those I have, and two or more horses for servants to ride, as we are to make the tour of Ireland…'. The fact that his wife 'brings me Fifty thousand pounds hard cash down, and will at her Father's and Aunt's death succeed to one hundred and fifty thousand more' was undoubtedly an incentive.[123]

Lord Doneraile paid over £150 for a coach bought in London and shipped to Ireland in 1775.[124] The coach is described as:

> *neatly run with raised Beads, painted Barrie Colour with Arms in handsome Ornaments, a handsome Border round the Pannells, the Beads Gilded, the Leather Japan'd & brass Beads all round it, lined with Spotted Manchester Velvet, the Seat Cloth with one row of fringe with Silk button hangers, Plate Glasses to slide in front, Glasses & Mahogany Shutters in the Doors, an Oval Glass & Cushion to the back, wainscott Trunks under the Seats, a carpet to the bottom, hung on a light strong Carriage with Iron Axletree screw'd at the Ends, wrought Boxes and patent Wheels with browhoops, upright Steel Springs, small hind Standards, Coachbox to take off, high Budget, the Carriage & Wheels painted the Colour of the Body & pick'd out green and white….*

In 1837 a Doneraile heir ordered ten harnesses (again in London) with 'silver embosd and chasd crests and coronets on do'.[125] But handsome carriages with silver trimmings were not just for the nobility and the rich. Dorothea Herbert vividly describes going to the Cashel Races in 1789 in their new coach, just arrived from Dublin, with 'four of the handsomest young Bay Horses in the Kingdom… really a Most beautiful Vehicle, Bottle Green adorned with a Quantity of Silver Plate, and the harnesses equally enrich'd with Silver… in short we were the Gaze and Astonishment of the Whole Race Course'.[126] No less impressed was the actor John O'Keeffe when, as a young boy at Trimleston Castle, County Meath, he saw the coach presented to Lord Trimleston by Marshal Saxe. Students from the drawing

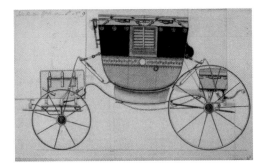

Fig. 24 – John Hutton, A design for a coach marked 'No. 9'. Hutton conducted a thriving coach-building business in Great Britain Street (now Parnell Street). Photo courtesy Mallett & Son (Antiques) Ltd., London and New York.

school in Dublin came to copy the paintings that decorated it.[127] The State Coach of the Lord Mayor of Dublin, built by the Dublin coachbuilder William Whitton in 1790 (recently restored), was greatly admired as it drove through the city and is decorated with paintings attributed to Vincent Waldré.[128] But coaches could be bought secondhand and advertisements such as one in *Pue's Occurrences* in June 1740 attach some importance to the colour, and often the fabric, of its lining, described as 'crimson dutch caffoy'.[129] Bishop Edward Synge's requirements for his new coach included some colour coordination: 'Blue Cloath for the lining – a fuller blue than the Servants Big-Coats. Get also a very handsome fringe for the Hammer-Cloth and a leather one for journeys', and 'good clever large pockets at the Doors, well bound and secure' (fig. 24).[130]

For the wealthy, moving from one house to another meant travelling as a small cavalcade with servants. Many, like the Leinsters, the Conollys and even the Delanys, took their carriages with them when they travelled to England.[131] When Lord and Lady Buttevant were travelling from Dublin to Castle Lyons in County Cork in 1738, he travelled with a friend in a chaise and six and his wife with her maid in a landau and six, 'with led horses alongside and three or four servants'.[132] Dean and Mrs Delany travelled from their Dublin home to that in County Down in three conveyances – they in their chaise, the cook and housemaid in the coach and four, and another maid 'in a car we have had made for marketing and carrying luggage when we travel'.[133] But sometimes the cavalcade was not so small. According to a newspaper report on the Marquis of Abercorn's month-long journey between Baronscourt, County Tyrone, and London, their suite consisted of thirty-three persons in a cavalcade of four carriages and ten outriders. The latter comprised grooms and footmen, whose job was to go in advance of the carriages to ensure that all was in order at the various inns at which they stayed: the major domo and cook would arrive at the inn in the morning.[134]

The expense of owning a coach included the provision of livery for servants such as the coachman, postillion and footmen. In 1767, the Duke of Leinster upgraded his footmen[135] in line with his ducal status, providing them with 'a Pair of black Worsted Shag Breeches… a fine Felt Hat with a Silver Chain Loop and Buttons and a Horse Hair Cockade'.[136] The Revd Robert King of Ballylin, County Offaly, in 1821 paid his coachman £12 per annum, 'with Hat, Coat, Breeches and Jackett & Trowsers & Waistcoat'.[137] Family papers give lists of liveries made for servants, the buttons of which were stamped with the family's crest. In 1812, nine dozen plated buttons were supplied on which were stamped the 'hand and dagger' of the Kirkpatrick crest of Donacomper, County Kildare. Other expenses included a tax on carriages: Lord Shannon paid a total of £68.5s.0d in 1800 for two four-wheeled carriages in Dublin and three in Castlemartyr.[138]

Before discussing the type of accommodation required by people like Lord Shannon for their horses and carriages in Dublin, it is interesting to look at the practical and important role played by the humble cart and carthorse in transporting fresh produce from country estates to houses in Dublin. An example is the constant flow of food from Carton to Leinster House in Dublin, detailed in a manuscript.[139] A mule departed from Carton at 10am each Monday, Wednesday and Friday carrying 'Rowls, Butter, Eggs, Fowl, Game &c and Sallading', returning the following day (f. 29). On Tuesday and Saturday mornings a cart and two horses brought meat, garden produce, bread, and anything else that was required (f. 27). The mule was 'never to go faster than a Walk', the saddle was to be kept in good condition and 'great care to be taken of [the mule's] Feet, in the Shoeing, &c.'. In both directions the loads were weighed and an account sent to Lord Kildare and to the clerk of the kitchen. Detailed instructions about when and what harnesses and bridles were to be worn by the cart horses are laid down (f. 54, f. 55), as are orders regarding letters going to Dublin: only those 'directed by the [by then] Dutchess [*sic*] of Leinster, Or marked E:L by her Grace or directed or marked L by me shall be carried to Dublin by the Carters to the Porter at Leinster House'. If these orders were disobeyed, the Duke imposed a fine on the farmer and the carter (f. 84). Worrying that fruit might be damaged in the cart during transportation, he dispatched a note to the gardener that in future it should be sent either with 'Joe' (by mule or horseback) or by a man on foot (a footman) on Mondays, Wednesdays and Fridays (f. 88)![140] At Leinster House, the carts used a separate gateway on Kildare Street (where the National Museum now stands) that led directly into the stable yard.

There was no shortage of space at Leinster House for carts, horses, mules and accompanying servants. In 1745, Richard Castle provided drawings for it for the 20th Earl, on which the stables are shown located to the east of the house, in the space between the forecourt and the southern boundary at Kildare Place (fig. 25).

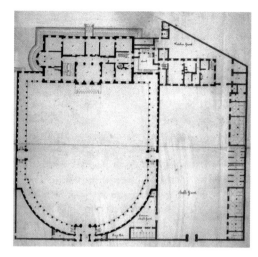

Fig. 25 – Richard Castle, Plan of Kildare (later Leinster) House (*c.* 1745) with stable yard where the National Museum of Ireland is now located. Photo courtesy Irish Architectural Archive.

Fig. 26 – A vignette from John Rocque, *A survey of the city, harbour, bay and environs of Dublin* (Dublin, 1757) shows the water tank at Kildare (later Leinster) House.

Access from the court is through a pedimented Ionic gateway in the screen wall,[141] and a separate gateway on Kildare Street gave access directly into the stable yard. This is not dissimilar to the arrangement at Trinity College's Provost's House, where the entrance to the yard was on the corner of Grafton Street.[142] The ground floor of the block at Leinster House contained vaulted stables and coach houses, while accommodation for male servants and hay lofts were on the first floor.[143] Of nineteen bays, the rounded tops of the seven central bays for carriages were rusticated, a theme that continued to each side in alternating windows and doors. The block contained stabling for twenty-six horses and six coaches, and in a separate 'common stable yard' between the curved wall of the colonnade and the wall onto Kildare Street, was a stable for eight cart horses and a cart house. A carriage wash in front of the stable block and a water tank outside the kitchen office block can be seen on John Rocque's map of 1756, and in his bird's-eye view of the house in 1757 (fig. 26).[144]

While most peers and members of parliament looking for a Dublin residence purchased ready-built townhouses, or built as part of a terrace, some, like Leinster House and the Provost's House, were free-standing, stone-built mansions set back from street level. Stables were to one side of the house or to the rear.[145] Because the house occupied a large plot, there was ample space for stables and outbuildings. It was the narrow terraced townhouse plot that was a challenge, onto which a building that included the required stable, coach house, loft, accommodation for servants, and access from a rear laneway, was incorporated. This building type, now known as a mews, is essentially British, originating at Covent Garden, London, in the 1630s, but became common in Dublin from the early eighteenth century.[146] Articles of agreement between Luke Gardiner and Primate Boulter, dated 1724, for a plot on Henrietta Street, on which stood three unfinished houses, stipulated that 'there shall be a back lane or street of at Least Twenty-two feet in Breadth for the passage of Coaches & Horses from Bolton-street… to the Coach-houses and Stables… belonging to the Premises'.[147] It was the usual practice to provide in the leases for stable lanes behind terraced rows of houses, as at Fitzwilliam Square.[148] But not everybody on Merrion Square wanted to share the back lane with his neighbours. William Brownlow took a 68-foot plot on the north side and built a house with a passage through to his coach house to one side, and in 1765 Lord

Mornington sought a 100-foot plot on which to build a house, with 'a Gateway of either side his house for the greater security thereof, and for the more convenient passage to his Stables as he intends to have no communication with the stable lane'. Mornington's approach came to nothing and he later established himself in Merrion Street.[149]

The Merrion Square plots were on average 30 feet in width and 290 feet in depth, providing a fairly long garden between house and mews building. Isaac Ware recommended paving the rear garden space, as it was confined between high walls and the rear wall of a coach house, stating that 'plants require a purer air than animals'.[150]   But townhouse gardens in Dublin are rather longer than those in London and are more suited to being planted. To many, the idea of gardening in town on a small patch was of little interest, particularly among those who had country residences, and town houses were frequently rented out during the 'season' or at other times during the year. However, the mews complex at 63 Merrion Square that has survived almost intact from the late eighteenth century contains a unique feature – a mews garden, separated from the main garden of the house by a brick wall (fig. 27). Its purpose remains a mystery. Giles Worsley had never heard of one, perhaps because 'the space between house and mews was seldom… long enough' in England, and suggested that it might have had a practical use, such as for drying clothes.[151] The brick-built two-storey mews retains the stalls with brick setts and a cobbled coachhouse and yard. Two coaches and up to six horses could be accommodated, with a small living area for servants and a hay loft.[152]

Fig. 27 – Mews building to rear of 63 Merrion Square, showing wall of mews garden. Photo courtesy the Irish Landmark Trust

A similar mews, though without the mews garden, is shown on a plan for a house on the west side of Sackville Street, Dublin, for William Gore, Bishop of Elphin, where accommodation is provided for eight horses and two coaches, with rooms for the coachman and servants over it.[153] A plan by Edward Lovett Pearce shows a three-bay townhouse from the rear of which, at basement level, an underground passage (beneath the garden) leads to what seems to be a laundry and yard: next to that and parallel to the site with a passage to one side, is the stable. Between the stable and the coachhouse is a yard with a wide gateway that gives access to the back lane.[154] An underground passage was not unusual: a house in Henrietta Street, Dublin, has a garden at ground floor level, under which is a passage that led to the mews. This was not unusual in London, where subterranean offices were sometimes built linking the two areas, with a terrace laid out over it.[155]

There were problems in having the house so close to the stables in town: one was aesthetic, the other practical. To make the view from the house more palatable, many well-known architects in Britain provided designs for decorative façades or screen walls with niches, but there is no indication that this was done in Ireland. From the evidence available, it would appear that those built on Merrion Square, at least, had an attractive façade to the main house: a two-storeyed red-brick building with a double-pile roof, a central doorway and small, subdivided sash windows with granite sills.[156] However, a Gothick Revival mews façade, complete with a castellated pediment, survives to the rear of 49 Merrion Square.

The Wide Streets Commission in 1794 was involved in a dispute arising from a house built by Graham Myers on the north side of St Stephen's Green, five feet back from the range of the house it replaced. This had the effect of shortening the distance between house and stables, and 'bringing the smell of the stables so near the eating parlour' that 'it may prevent the sale or setting from that circumstance alone'.[157] The Earl of Orrery was nothing if not direct when he wrote to the Bishop of Cork (Clayton) on 11 December 1736 to congratulate him on his new house in St Stephen's Green (now part of Iveagh House) which he visited in the company of Richard Castle, its architect:

> *Your Palace, my Lord, appears finely upon Paper, and to shew You that the whole pleases me, I even admire your Coal Cellars… but however good your Hearing or Sight may be delighted, I am in some Fear that your Smell will not be regal'd from your Stables unless you shoft your Garden as soon as possible with Roses, Lilies, and All the Flowers that are celebrated in Song. This inconvenience might be prevented if your Lordship can purchase a little more Ground behind your House; but so that the Stable has a beautiful Cornish, Signor Cassells does not seem to care where it stands.*[158]

It seemed to have been of little importance that living in the mews might have been unhealthy for those servants who were obliged to do so. Accommodation there was fairly standard and sparsely furnished, with one room for the coachman while the postillion and stable hands slept in the hayloft.

Coachmen tended to be engaged directly by a master for their ability at the reins, as they were responsible for the safety of their passengers and of the equipage. They were also expected to have an extensive knowledge of farriery. The coachman had the difficult job of maintaining his distance from weaving vehicles, sometimes conducted by drunken drivers, and protecting the carriage from damage.[159] He was the most senior of the lower male servants, in charge of the stables, the postillions, grooms and stable hands. His was a distinctive livery of greatcoat, top hat and boots and he carried the ubiquitous whip. He and his staff generally started work at 6am, dressing the horses, washing and cleaning the carriage and harness, and at the appointed hour, he would have the carriage at the door of the house, facing in the appropriate direction.[160] He was expected to drive at a uniform pace of between four and eight miles per hour, as specified at the start of the journey by his master.[161] In severe weather coachmen suffered cruelly, waiting for their masters to emerge from social gatherings.

Sometimes the coachman might be expected to wait at the dinner table. This happened regularly in town, when use was made of a smaller number of staff than would be the case in the country. The coachman would be given an hour or so to wash down the carriage and tend the horses, which frequently left him little time to wash himself. All too often the gastronomic delights of the dinner might be accompanied by the odour of the stables. Wages for a coachman in the latter third of the eighteenth century varied between twelve and twenty guineas per year. Grooms were paid on average ten pounds and postillions received six to seven pounds, usually with a wig and hat supplied. Sadly the value placed on the lives of the younger members of staff, postillions and stable hands, is underlined by the following report that appeared in *Pue's Occurrences* in 1743:

> *Yesterday morning, early [July 1] a fire broke out in the stables belonging to the Rt Hon the Lord Bellfield, in Strand Street, which burnt with great fury; but with the timely assistance of the water engines it was happily extinguished. Two boys who lay in the hayloft were so miserably burnt, that they died in a few hours after.*[162]

Thankfully there is no evidence to suggest that any such accidents took place at the Provost's House Stables in either their original form or in those built by Darley.

CONCLUSION

In this essay the architecture of the stable has been seen from as early as the 1630s as an opportunity for display and power: Thomas Wentworth set about building new stables at Dublin Castle that he expected would outdo those provided for the King by Inigo Jones; at one of his country houses in 1662 the newly-created Duke of Ormonde planned to replace the old stables with a building similar to a royal hunting lodge in England, and Lord Conway in 1671 sent drawings to his agent in Antrim as models for his new stables there. The first half of the eighteenth century was dominated by the Palladian plan, in which the house was linked by curved colonnades or walls to pavilions in one of which the stables were located. Diocletian and *oeil-de-boeuf* windows, cupolas and clocks became architectural motifs on stable buildings during this time, and the vaulted stable, in designs by Pearce and Castle, was a particularly Irish feature. The second half of the century saw the stable emerge as a building in its own right, often quadrangular in shape, built at a remove from the house and dressed in a variety of styles. Morrison's plans for those at Howth Castle, drawn up at the same time as the Provost's House Stables, demonstrate that combinations of styles were also possible.

We have looked at the many roles of the horse: as part of the military, as a gift, a racer and a hunter, and as a means of transport. Moving their owners from one place to another was the main function of the horse in the city and a great deal of money could be spent, not just on procuring a horse of a particular colour and shape, but on its equipage, in an effort to outdo everybody else. The Provost's House Stables was built to accommodate horses that had such a functional role, for riding about town, or for drawing carriages. Conscious of the building's street façade, Darley provided one that creates its own classical, though rather sober, architectural statement. He designed a building that was competent and functional: at the time of its design, the mews building, with its modest architectural vocabulary, was well established to serve town houses, when stone-built, free-standing houses, like the Provost's House, in the centre of Dublin were no longer being built.

Little is known of the earlier Provost's stables (built in the early 1760s), as Edward McParland has pointed out. Did a modicum of the care and attention that was lavished on the building and the superb decoration of the Provost's House by the man responsible, the *bon vivant* Provost Francis Andrews, extend to his stables? No contemporary accounts of social occasions at the house have as yet come to light, but surely, on those infrequent occasions when he was not abroad,[163] Andrews entertained his many friends, among whom was the Lord Lieutenant, the 4th Duke of Bedford, in style. We can only imagine the scene as carriages, having deposited guests at the door, lined up in the spacious forecourt to await departure, while the coachmen, footmen and postillions chattered and gossiped in the adjoining stable yard.

The author would like to thank the following who, in various ways, assisted her research: Anne Crookshank, Antoinette Dornan, Frank Farrell, Jane Fenlon, Livia Hurley, William Laffan, Elizabeth Mayes, Camilla McAleese, Mary McGrath, John Montague, Kevin Mulligan, Elmarie Nagle and Guy St John Williams. Particular thanks to Edward McParland for his much-valued suggestions, to Desmond FitzGerald, Knight of Glin for his active support, and to Yvonne Scott and Rachel Moss for their patient and meticulous editing of the text.

1   Quoted in Leo F. McNamara, 'Some matters touching Dromoland: letters of father and son, 1758–59', *North Munster Antiquarian Journal*, 27 (1986), pp 62–70.

2   Quoted from Toby Barnard, *Making the grand figure: lives and possessions in Ireland 1641–1770* (New Haven and London, 2004), p. 227.

3   Quoted from Mairead Dunlevy, *Dublin Barracks: a brief history of Collins Barracks, Dublin* (Dublin, 2002), p. 17.

4   Richard, Viscount Molesworth, *A short course of standing rules for the government and conduct of an army, designed for, or in the field* (Dublin, 1745), pp 142–6.

5   With no information about stables at the Castle prior to this time, it is unclear if a separate stable for Wentworth's bodyguard was an innovation.

6   David Howarth, *Images of rule: art and politics in the English Renaissance, 1485–1649* (Basingstoke, 1997), p. 198. The church may be the one that existed on the same site as the present chapel, and can be seen on Rocque's map of 1756.

7   *Ibid.*, p. 207.

8   Sir William Brereton, *Travels in Holland, the United Provinces, England, Scotland and Ireland 1634–35*, Edward Hawkins (ed.), (Manchester, 1844), quoted in C.L.

Falkiner, *Illustrations of Irish history and topography mainly of the seventeenth century* (London, 1904), p. 402; Giles Worsley, *The British stable* (New Haven and London, 2004), p. 45.

[9] Illustrated in Edward McParland, *Public architecture in Ireland 1680–1760* (New Haven and London, 2001), p. 92, fig. 111.

[10] J.B. Maguire, 'Seventeenth-century plans of Dublin Castle', *Journal of the Royal Society of Antiquaries of Ireland*, 104 (1974), pp 5–14. My thanks to Rachel Moss for this reference.

[11] My thanks to John Montague for bringing this to my attention.

[12] The water was conveniently available to clean both horses and stables.

[13] Rolf Loeber, 'The rebuilding of Dublin Castle: 30 critical years 1661–1690', *Studies* (Spring, 1980), pp 45–69. On the survey plan of the stable or lower Castle Yard of 1684 by William Robinson, illustrated on p. 67, three stables (built before 1688) can be seen to the east, and a range of coach houses facing onto Dame Lane. These buildings can also be seen in NLI MS 2789, f. 46 (1769, copied 1804). My thanks to Edward McParland for these references.

[14] McParland, *Public architecture*, p. 94.

[15] *Ibid.*, p. 98.

[16] Now Collins Barracks.

[17] Dunlevy, *Dublin Barracks*, pp 13, 17, 19; illustrations 8a and 8b, p. 18.

[18] James Douet, *British barracks 1600–1914* (London, 1998), p. 32. According to Douet, nineteenth-century barracks 'tended to have stalls backing onto an axial corridor running the length of the building'.

[19] According to Worsley, the term is often confused with an 'exercising ring' which he defines as 'a circular or similar shaped covered riding ring usually with open sides' and a 'covered ride' which he states is a 'long straight enclosed space usually with turning areas at the end'. Worsley, *The British stable*, p. 283, n. 1.

[20] Richard Berenger, *The history and art of horsemanship. By Richard Berenger,… In two volumes* (London, 1771), I, pp 182–3.

[21] Joan Thirsk, *Horses in early modern England: for service, for pleasure, for power* (Reading, 1978), p. 16.

[22] 'Privy Council Papers 1640–1707', Gilbert MS 205, f. 73–4.

[23] The buildings close by on Rocque's map are possibly the stables by Burgh, one range of which was built in 1714, and which were either replaced or added to, in 1746, by

the 'new stables, hay lofts and granaries' built to designs by Arthur Jones Nevill 'near Thomas Burgh's riding house below the Lower Yard'. McParland, *Public architecture*, pp 98, 103, and fig. 119, p. 95.

24   Quoted in Maguire, 'Seventeenth-century plans of Dublin Castle', p. 11.

25   McParland, *Public architecture*, p. 125.

26   Dunlevy, *Dublin Barracks*, p. 19; Molesworth, *A short course*, pp 142–6.

27   See article by Kenneth Ferguson, 'The riding house with a steeple: a puzzle connected with Dublin Barracks in the age of Lord Chesterfield', *The Irish Sword*, 25: 100 (Winter, 2006), pp 121–36.

28   Douet, *British barracks 1600–1914*, p. 33.

29   Henry Heaney (ed.), *A Scottish Whig in Ireland 1835–38: the Irish journals of Robert Graham of Redgorton* (Dublin, 1999), p. 94.

30   Worsley, *The British stable*, p. 60.

31   'Map of Carrickbeg, Co. Waterford [*sic*] belonging to James duke of Ormond by John Taylor', NLI MS 16B.12 (12). These were later converted to army barracks. My thanks to Jane Fenlon for this information.

32   Jane Fenlon, 'The decorative plasterwork at Ormond Castle: a unique survival', *Architectural History*, 41 (1998), pp 67–81.

33   R.C. Simington (ed.), *The Civil Survey, A.D. 1654–56*, 6… Kilkenny city & liberties (part)…, (Dublin, 1942), p. 534. My thanks to Jane Fenlon for this reference.

34   Rolf Loeber, 'Irish country houses and castles of the late Caroline period: an unremembered past recaptured', *Quarterly Bulletin of the Irish Georgian Society*, 16: 1 & 2 (Jan.–June, 1973), p. 44.

35   Letter from Duke of Ormonde from Whitehall to Sir William Flower, 3 April 1668. Bodleian Library, Oxford, Carte MS 219, no. 98. My thanks to Jane Fenlon for this reference.

36   Thirsk, *Horses*, p. 16, n. 76.

37   Quoted in Loeber, 'Irish country houses', p. 44.

38   Toby Barnard, 'The political, material and mental culture of the Cork settlers, *c.* 1650–1700' in P. O'Flanagan and C.G. Buttimer (eds), *Cork history and society* (Dublin, 1993), pp 309–65. Irish horses called 'hobbies' were raced in England against the King's horses in 1532; see Brian de Breffny (ed.), *Ireland: a cultural encyclopaedia* (London, 1983), p. 110. According to the *OED* they were 'a small or middle-sized horse; an ambling or racing horse', the earliest references to it are as an

Irish breed and later as Welsh and Scottish. The edition consulted is: *The Complete Edition of the Oxford English Dictionary* (Oxford, 1971).

[39]   Edward MacLysaght, *Irish life in the XVII century* (Dublin, 1950, 1979 edn.), pp 143–4.

[40]   Barnard, *Making the grand figure*, p. 227.

[41]   John Ainsworth, *The Inchiquin Manuscripts* (Dublin, 1961), p. 511. The will is dated 6 April 1672.

[42]   Mrs Delany (when she was Mrs Pendarves) said of Sir Arthur Gore of Newton Gore, County Mayo, in 1732 that his 'dogs and horses are as dear to him as his children'. Quoted in Constantia Maxwell, *The stranger in Ireland* (London, 1954, Dublin edn. 1979), p. 141.

[43]   Quoted in 'Report on The Huntsman's Lodge & Dog Kennels, Fota Island' (Cork, 2003), compiled by Clare Hogan and Livia Hurley.

[44]   Barnard, 'Cork settlers', pp 309–65.

[45]   Quoted in *ibid*., pp 309–65.

[46]   J. Greig (ed.), *The diaries of a duchess: extracts from the diaries of the first duchess of Northumberland 1716–76* (London, 1926), entry dated 27 Sept. 1771.

[47]   According to Douet in *British barracks*, Bastide's plan, which shows 150 stables, is equal to three troop of horses, p 32; Dunlevy quotes *The secret history and memoirs of the barracks in Ireland* (London, 1747) where a troop of horse consists of 36 horsemen or troopers who, with their superior officers, numbered 43. Dunlevy, *Dublin Barracks*, p. 60, n. 36.

[48]   Apparently it was suggested that, because of its vastness, Conway had to enlarge his house 'to make it suitable to that fine building'. Loeber, 'Irish country houses', p. 44.

[49]   Illustrated in Worsley, *The British stable*, p. 88.

[50]   Another architect was involved in the building of these stables – an Englishman, William Dodson, who came to Ireland prior to 1659. Dodson provided various proposals for additions to Phoenix House where, according to Loeber, he 'finished the stables'. Rolf Loeber, *A biographical dictionary of architects in Ireland, 1600–1720* (London, 1981). Dodson was contracted to build a wall enclosing Phoenix Park which, as Maurice Craig points out, 'he farmed out for one-third the price, and which fell down before it was paid for'. Maurice Craig, *Dublin 1660–1860* (Dublin, 1969), p. 15.

[51]   Worsley, *The British stable*, pp 94, 96; illustrations 81, 95 and 95.

[52]   Loeber, *A biographical dictionary*, p. 61.

53 Loeber, 'Irish country houses', pp 30–1, frontispiece, plate 8. The 'bawn' as this type of enclosure was known in Ireland from the sixteenth century, was used to describe the location of horses in an inventory of Baskin, County Dublin, 1734: '2 horses in Baun'. TCD MS 3575/16.

54 Quoted in T.F. Crofton Croker (ed.), *The tour of the French traveller M. de la Boullaye le Gouz in Ireland, 1644* (London, 1837), p. 132.

55 Quoted in Loeber, 'Irish country houses', p. 44.

56 Worsley, *The British stable*, pp 131–2.

57 Howard Colvin and Maurice Craig (eds), *Architectural drawings in the library of Elton Hall by Sir John Vanbrugh and Sir Edward Lovett Pearce* (Oxford, 1964), Stillorgan Album; Worsley, *The British stable*, p. 138.

58 Vaulted stables designed by Castle can be seen at Gill Hall, County Down, Strokestown House, County Roscommon, Bellinter and Ardbraccan, both in County Meath, Russborough, County Wicklow, in an unexecuted plan for Headfort, County Meath and in plans for Leinster House, Dublin.

59 Worsley, *The British stable*, p. 149.

60 The stable quadrangle can be seen on an anonymous and undated garden plan, *Ichnographia Dromolan*. The plan is illustrated in Finola O'Kane, 'Leamaneh and Dromoland: the O'Brien ambition', part II, *Irish Architectural and Decorative Studies*, 7 (2004), pp 80–105, plate I. The stables were built in the Palladian style, and the reason why Sir Edward went against the trend in 1736 of stable pavilions linked to the house may have been because he had ambitions to build a new house at this time.

61 The album is in the National Library of Ireland (NLI MS 2791), photocopy in Irish Architectural Archive. Many of the drawings are by John Aheron, to whom the 1736 stable at Dromoland is attributed.

62 The stables at Fonthill House, Wiltshire, built in the 1630s, had *oeil-de-boeuf* windows. Worsley, *The British stable*, p. 77.

63 It was because they obstructed the view from the house that they were demolished in 1732 and a new block, identical in plan, was designed by William Kent. Worsley, *The British stable*, pp 128–9.

64 Frances Cobbe, *Life of Frances Power Cobbe as told by herself* (London, 1904 edn.), p.32.

65 Worsley, *The British stable*, p. 41.

66 *Ibid.*, p. 42.

67 Howard Colvin and John Newman (eds), *Of building. Roger North's writings on*

architecture (Oxford, 1981), p. 96.

[68]   John Lawrence, *A philosophical and practical treatise on horses, and on the man towards the brute creation* (London, 1796–8), pp 37, 46; James Clark, *A treatise on the prevention of diseases incidental to horses* (Edinburgh, 1781, 2nd edn. 1790), pp 19–47.

[69]   Worsley, *The British stable*, p. 44.

[70]   Quoted in *ibid.*, pp 44–5.

[71]   Hugh Montgomery Massingberd and Christopher Simon Sykes, *Great houses of Ireland* (London, 1999), p. 16.

[72]   Mark Bence-Jones, *A guide to Irish country houses* (London, 1978, 1988 edn.), p. 78.

[73]   Dating prior to 1817.

[74]   A circular 'riding house' (as a plaque on its entrance informs the visitor) with a cast-iron colonnade, built in the mid-nineteenth century, can be seen at Russborough, County Wicklow, while the remains of one are to be seen at Lissadell, County Sligo, according to the National Inventory for Architectural Heritage, Registration no. 32400809.

[75]   As at Rockingham, County Roscommon, designed by John Nash (from 1810), the house described as 'isolated in a smooth sea of shaven lawns'. Gordon Wheeler, 'John Nash and the building of Rockingham, County Roscommon' in H.M. Colvin and John Harris (eds), *The country seat: studies in the history of the British country house presented to Sir John Summerson on his 65th birthday together with a select bibliography of his published writings* (London, 1970), pp 169–5.

[76]   Ann Martha Rowan (ed.), *The architecture of Richard Morrison and William Vitruvius Morrison* (Dublin, 1989), pp 106–7.

[77]   Worsley, *The British stable*, p. 124.

[78]   Kevin Mulligan, 'Ballyfin: an architectural history' (unpublished report for Ballyfin Demesne Ltd.), 2002. Among others were Castle Dillon, Castle Upton, Carriglas, and Castlecoole.

[79]   Christopher Powell, *Stables and stable blocks* (Buckinghamshire, 1991), p. 20.

[80]   An observation on the Irish by a writer in 1719, quoted in P. Livingstone, *The Fermanagh story* (Enniskillen, 1969), p. 121.

[81]   Stanislaus Lynch, 'Hunting in Ireland' in Noel Phillips Browne (ed.), *The horse in Ireland* (London, 1967), pp 134–48.

[82]   Maxwell, *The stranger in Ireland*, p. 121.

[83]   Colin A. Lewis, *Hunting in Ireland: an historical and geographical analysis* (London,

1975), p. 44.

84 'The Killruddery Hunt' was also a well-known song commemorating a foxhunt in County Wicklow in 1744.

85 Quoted in Constantia Maxwell, *Country and town in Ireland under the Georges* (London, 1940, 1949 edn.), p. 33.

86 NAI, Meath Papers, K/1/2 1827–33, p. 210.

87 Quoted in Valerie Pakenham, *The big house in Ireland* (London, n.d.), pp 129–30.

88 'Hunting Journal of Hayes St Leger, 4th Viscount Doneraile, Oct. 1837–Mar. 1838', Doneraile Papers, NLI MS 34,143 (1).

89 Doneraile Papers, information taken from the abstract to the papers.

90 Tom Conolly is referred to as the 'Father of the Turf Club' in Fergus A. D'Arcy, *Horses, lords and racing men: the Turf Club 1790–1990* (Kildare, 1991), p. 6; and as 'the type and pattern of the Irish gentleman and sportsman' in D. Bourke, Earl of Mayo, and W.B. Boulton, *History of the Kildare Hunt* (London, 1913), p. 19.

91 Bourke and Boulton, *History of the Kildare Hunt*, p. 36.

92 Quoted in *ibid.*, pp 31–2.

93 See Anne Crookshank and the Knight of Glin, *Ireland's painters 1600–1940* (New Haven and London, 2002), p. 89.

94 Lewis, *Hunting in Ireland*, p. 44.

95 Cobbe, *Life*, p. 17.

96 Pakenham, *Big house*, p. 126.

97 Bourke and Boulton, *History of the Kildare Hunt*, p. 25.

98 Barnard, *Making the grand figure*, p. 238.

99 Letter from Lady Louisa Conolly to Tom Conolly, 12 April 1772 or 1773, Bunbury Letters, IAA 97/84. My thanks to the Castletown Foundation for permission to use this material.

100 For the members of the hunt, Lord Burlington designed a banqueting room at Charlton, known as Foxhall; a gilded fox surmounting a flagstaff was erected in front of it 'to show the "southerly wind", so dear to fox-hunters'. T.J. Bennett, 'Charlton and the Charlton Hunt: a sketch of the olden time', *Sussex Archaeological Collections*, 15 (1863), pp 74–82.

101 Letter from Robert Taylor to Sir Thomas Taylor, 25 Feb 1742. Headfort Papers, NLI PC 12,552.

102 Maxwell, *Country and town*, p. 25.

[103]   James Kelly (ed.), *The letters of Lord Chief Baron Edward Willes to the Earl of Warwick 1757–62* (Aberystwyth, 1990), p. 69.

[104]   Ronan Lynch, *The Kirwans of Castlehacket, County Galway* (Dublin, 2006), p. 48; Guy St John Williams, *The racing lodges of the Curragh* (Kildare, 1997), frontispiece 'Map of the Curragh of Kildare shewing the Race Courses Gentlemens Seats &c Accurately described, surveyed by H Walker 1807'.

[105]   Unexecuted design for hunting box for 1st Earl of Charlemont, Roxborough Castle, County Tyrone, by Sir William Chambers in 1768. Photocopy, IAA, Photograph Boxes.

[106]   Castlecoole, County Fermanagh, Plan for a… Hunting Lodge and Offices for the Earl of Belmore by Richard Morrison. IAA, Photograph Boxes; Rowan (ed.), *Architecture*, p. 184. The plan of the lodge bears a resemblance to that of Carriglas, County Longford, by James Gandon.

[107]   Quoted in MacLysaght, *Irish life*, p. 145.

[108]   Maxwell, *Country and town*, p. 31; J.L. McCracken, 'The social structure and social life, 1714–60' in T.W. Moody & W.E. Vaughan, *New history of Ireland*, 4, *Eighteenth-century Ireland* (Oxford, 1986), pp 31–56.

[109]   Barnard, *Making the grand figure*, p. 228.

[110]   Barnard, 'Cork settlers', pp 309–65. In the early eighteenth century Queen Anne endowed a plate of 100 guineas annually at the Curragh.

[111]   Brian FitzGerald, *Correspondence of Emily Duchess of Leinster (1731–1814)* (Dublin, 1949), p. 61.

[112]   Letter from Lady Louisa Conolly to Lady Sarah Bunbury, 3 May 1768. Bunbury Letters, IAA 94/136.

[113]   McCracken, 'The social structure and social life, 1714–60', pp 31–56.

[114]   Barnard, *Making the grand figure*, p. 229.

[115]   Grania R. O'Brien, *These my friends and forebears: the O'Briens of Dromoland* (Clare, 1991), p. 61.

[116]   According to local lore, Sir Edward, who suffered from gout, could watch in comfort the local point-to-point races that finished below the gazebo. McNamara, 'Some matters touching Dromoland', pp 62–70.

[117]   *Faulkner's Dublin Journal*, 10–13 July 1742.

[118]   Quoted in McNamara, 'Some matters touching Dromoland', pp 62–70.

[119]   John McVeagh (ed.), *Richard Pococke's Irish tours* (Dublin, 1995), p. 41.

[120]   Angélique Day (ed.), *Letters from Georgian Ireland* (Belfast,1991), pp 25–6.

[121]   Letter from Lady Caroline Dawson to her sister Lady Louisa Stuart, May 1784, in Mrs G. Clark (ed.), *Gleanings from an old portfolio*, 3 vols (Edinburgh, 1895) 1.

[122]   Barnard, *Making the grand figure*, pp 231–2.

[123]   Thomas U. Sadlier, 'Letter from Edward, 2nd Earl of Aldborough, to his agent at Belan', *Journal of the County Kildare Archaeological Society*, 6 (1912–14), pp 333–4.

[124]   Invoice to The Right Honble Lord Doneraile from John Wright & Co. London. Doneraile Papers, NLI MS 34,112(7), 5 Oct. 1775.

[125]   Accounts for household and personal, gardens and livery 1837–39. Doneraile Papers, NLI MS 34, 120.

[126]   Dorothea Herbert, *Retrospections of Dorothea Herbert 1770–1806* (London 1929–30, 1988 edn.), p. 217–8.

[127]   Maxwell, *Country and town*, p. 49.

[128]   See Philip McEvansoneya, 'A colourful spectacle restored: the State coach of the lord mayor of Dublin', *Irish Arts Review Yearbook*, 17 (2001), pp 80–7.

[129]   *Pue's Occurrences*, 10–14 June 1740, no. 48; *ibid.*, 30 Dec.–3 Jan. 1718–9, 16: 1; *ibid.*, 27–30 Jan. 1739, no. 9; *ibid.*, 26 Feb. 1757, no. 17, 'painted in the Mozaick way….'. On the subject of colour, Lord and Lady Kildare supervised the building being carried out at Carton in the late 1740s to early 1750s, 'riding around in a pea-green chaise', according to Brian FitzGerald, *Lady Louisa Conolly 1743–1821* (London, 1950), p. 14.

[130]   Letter 20, 11 July 1747 in Marie-Louise Legg (ed.), *The Synge Letters 1746–1752* (Dublin, 1996), pp 51–2.

[131]   FitzGerald, *Lady Louisa Conolly*, pp 14–15; the Delanys took with them in 1747 'a light 4-wheeled chaise… besides our coach'.

[132]   Maxwell, *Country and town*, pp 59–60.

[133]   Day (ed.), *Letters*, p. 203.

[134]   Quoted in Lord Ernest Hamilton, *Old days and new* (London, 1923), p. 35.

[135]   Part of the footman's duty was to ride on the outside of the coach.

[136]   'Rules for the government of the Marquis of Kildare's (Duke of Leinster's) household 1763–1773', Alnwick Castle Archives, Northumberland, MS 670, f. 69.

[137]   Peter Somerville-Large, *The Irish country house* (London, 1995), p. 230.

[138]   Shannon Papers, PRONI D2707/B15.

[139]   Kildare House, Dublin, called Leinster House after the dukedom was conferred on Lord Kildare in 1766. 'Rules for the government of the Marquis of Kildare's (Duke

of Leinster's) household 1763–1773' Alnwick Castle Archives, Northumberland, MS 670; Patricia McCarthy, 'Vails and travails: how Lord Kildare kept his household in order', *Irish Architectural and Decorative Studies*, 6 (2003), pp 120–39.

140   Sometimes referred to as 'running' footmen, part of whose duties was to run errands, often of great distances, taking short cuts across the countryside. Part of their employer's equipage, he would run before the carriage to prepare an inn or lodging for the arrival of his master.

141   A similar gateway (blind) was symmetrically placed on the west wall of the courtyard.

142   My thanks to Edward McParland for this information.

143   David G. Griffin and Caroline Pegum, *Leinster House* (Dublin, 2000), p. 19.

144   *Ibid.*, frontispiece, and p. 69, n. 7.

145   The Duke of Ormonde's London residence, Ormonde House, was at numbers 9, 10 and 11 St James's Square. An undated document shows that among his servants was a 'gentleman of the horse, 2 coachmen, 8 other stablemen and a 'chasseur' or huntsman.' The stables behind contained 20 horses, 5 coaches and 14 hunting dogs. F.H.W. Sheppard (general ed.), *Survey of London XXIX, Parish of St James, Westminster*, (London, 1960), Part 1, p. 119.

146   A plan, dated 1639, for a house in Amsterdam shows a mews entered from the rear, and is illustrated in Worsley, *The British stable*, p. 112. In Edinburgh, at Charlotte Square, many of the houses preferred a garden without a mews, but there are clusters of mews buildings located nearby that were rented by owners of houses on the square.

147   'Old Dublin Mansion-houses', *The Irish Builder* (15 June 1893), pp 136–7.

148   Mary Bryan, 'Fitzwilliam Square garden and its commissioners', *Irish Architectural and Decorative Studies*, 4 (2001), pp 79–101.

149   Siuban Barry, 'Merrion Square: a documentary and architectural study', BA dissertation, Trinity College Dublin (1977).

150   Quoted in Andrew Byrne, *Bedford Square: an architectural* study (London, 2001), p. 49.

151   E-mail correspondence from Giles Worsley to author, 21 Oct. 2004.

152   The mews has been recently restored by the Irish Landmark Trust and the living accommodation will be used for holiday rental. The stables will be retained and used by An Garda Siochána Mounted Unit.

153   Articles of agreement between George Darley of Dublin to William Gore, Bishop of Elphin, 12 Sept. 1769. Killadoon Papers, NLI MS 36,013 (1).

154 Colvin and Craig, *Architectural drawings in the library of Elton Hall*, cat. no. 65, unsigned and undated. My thanks to Edward McParland for drawing my attention to this.

155 Todd Longstaffe-Gowan, *The London town garden 1740–1840* (London, c. 2001), p. 44.

156 Nicola Matthews, 'Merrion Square' in *The Georgian squares of Dublin: an architectural history* (Dublin, 2006), pp 56–87.

157 Wide Streets Commissioners Minutes, Dublin City Library and Archive, Pearse Street, 12, p. 115. My thanks to Conor Lucey for bringing this to my attention.

158 Countess of Cork and Orrery (ed.), *The Orrery Papers*, 2 vols (London, 1903), I, pp 177–8.

159 E.S. Turner, *What the butler saw: 250 years of the servant problem* (London, 1962, 2001 edn.), p. 174.

160 It was considered an ill-managed household if the carriage had to be turned in the street.

161 Turner, *What the butler saw*, p. 175.

162 *Pue's Occurrences*, 28 June –2 July 1743, no. 53.

163 Edward McParland, 'Cherishing a Palladian masterpiece: the Provost's House, Trinity College, Dublin – II', *Country Life*, 160: 4138 (21 Oct. 1976), pp 1106–09.

Fig. 1 – St Patrick. BL Royal 17B.XLIII, f. 132v.

ST PATRICK'S WELL

Rachel Moss

Full fifty times Pat drank at the shrine
Of his titular saint – his skin full of wine;
Which made the saint debtor – so to bring accounts even,
On the 17th of March he snatch'd him to Heav'n.[1]

Just off the tree-lined pathway to the Provost's House Stables is a narrow vault that extends under Nassau Street, close to its junction with Dawson Street. Housed within this vault is a well, reputed to be St Patrick's Well, a once famous ancient focal point for St Patrick's Day revelry in the capital city.

Of the roughly one hundred holy wells recorded in Dublin, six are dedicated to St Patrick.[2] Foundation myths are recorded for several of these and one, probably created in the twelfth century, is thought to relate to the Nassau Street well. The account is found in chapter LXX of Jocelin of Furness' *Life of St Patrick*, which dates to *c.*1185/6:

And Saint Patrick, while abiding in this village [Dublin], was entertained at the house of a woman who often in his presence complained of the want of fresh water. For the river that ran near it was, by the flowing in of the tide of the sea, made wholly salt of taste; nor before the return thereof could any fresh water be obtained, unless drawn at a great distance. But the saint, who continually thirsted after God, the living fountain, compassionated the grievance of his hostess and of the multitude then newly born unto Christ, and, the rather that they might the more ardently pant toward the fountain of life, thought he fit to show its virtue. Therefore on the morrow he went unto a certain place, and in the presence of many standing around he prayed, and touched the earth with the Staff of Jesus, and in the name of the Lord produced from it a clear fountain. Thus with the staff in the hand of his preacher Saint Patrick did the Lord renew the miracle which of old time he had deigned to work by the rod in the hand of Moses striking the rock; there the rock twice struck flowed forth abundant waters; here the earth once pierced poured forth a pure fountain. And this is the fountain of Dublinia, wide in its stream, plenteous in its course, sweet to the taste, which, as is said, healeth many infirmities, and even to this day is rightly called the fountain of Saint Patrick.[3]

Jocelin's *Life* is the first to mention any association between the saint and Dublin, and his assertion, in another section of the *Life*, that Patrick came to the place when it was already inhabited by Vikings should be sufficient basis to doubt the veracity of his account.[4] The description of the well, however, would seem to confirm that by the twelfth century it was already a place of veneration, and one that was noted for the quality and abundance of its water.

During the Middle Ages the well would have been located a little outside the city walls close to All Hallows, a priory of Augustinian canons. The Augustinians were an order not averse to the promotion of pilgrimage: priories were often located at sites with important pilgrimage associations, such as St Patrick's Purgatory (Donegal), Mona Incha (Tipperary) and Ballinskelligs (Kerry), while a number of Augustinian houses, such as Trim (Meath), enjoyed revenue brought in through the veneration of 'miraculous' statues. It is possible, then, that the canons may have been involved in the perpetuation of the sacred associations of the well at All Hallows, although there is no direct evidence to support this.

Following the Dissolution, the lands that had formerly belonged to the priory were, in 1592, given by Queen Elizabeth I to the newly-founded College of the Holy Trinity. In a description of the property granted to the College at this time, the southern boundary is described as 'the lane that leads to St Patrick's Well to the south of the monastery of the Blessed Virgin' (*vanella qui ducit ad fontem Saint Patricci ex parte australi usque ad terram predictam nuper monasterii beate Marie Virginus).*[5]

Despite its proximity to a College with such a strong Anglican ethos, the well appears to have reached the apogee of its popularity in the early seventeenth century, a period during which devotions at holy wells across the country enjoyed something of a renaissance, with well houses erected over existing wells, and some 'new' wells established for the first time.[6] Our earliest and most comprehensive accounts of the pattern there both come from Barnabe Rich, an English writer and soldier who spent the latter part of his life in Dublin. It should be noted that Rich was not an altogether objective observer, believing, as he did, that all of Ireland's difficulties were due to the religion of the people and to the lack of firmness on the part of the English government!

In his *A New Description of Ireland*, published *c.*1610, Rich described the pattern day thus:

> On the East part [of Dublin] they haue Sai. Patrick's well, the water whereof, although it be generally reputed to bee very hot, yet the very prime of the perfection, is upon 17. of March, which is Sai. Patrick's day, and vpon this day, the water is more holy than it is all the yeare after, or else the inhabitants of Dublin are more foolish vpon this day, than they be al the yeare after. For vpon that day thither they wil run by heapes, men, women and children, and there, first performing certain superstitious ceremonies, they drinke of the water; and when they are returned to their owne homes, for nine days after, they will sit and tell what wonderfull things haue bin wrought by the operation of the water of Sa. Patrick's Well.[7]

Two years later in his *A Catholycke conference between Syr Thady Mac Mareall, a popish priest of Waterford and Patrick Playne, a young student of Trinity Colledge by Dublyne in Ireland*, Rich's character, Sir Thady, compares the pilgrimage to the well to similar devotional exercises taking place at St Patrick's Purgatory (Donegal), Holy Cross (Tipperary) and St Sunday's Well (Cork):

> But let me draw somewhat near to your college it self: are you not eye witness how every 17th March what flocking there is of men, women and children to that same holy sanctified pool, Saint Patrick's well. I hope you do not think the whole multitude that do so yearly frequent the place to be stark mad, to come running hither so thick, if they did not find some sanctity in the water? I warrant you they are not so arrant fools, as a number of those that do use to take tobacco, that will still be stuffing themselves with smoke, but upon vain conceit.[8]

Given the 'heaps' of 'stark mad' Catholics 'running thick' so close to the College, it is interesting how silent the early College records are on the well and the activities around it. A memorandum entered into the College Register in 1665 notes that the 'way' leading to the well had been improved at the expense of the City, and then states that this is only being recorded because the College had formerly taken responsibility for it.[9] The sense that one gets of the College distancing itself from the well is further strengthened five years later when, 'in consideration of the want of water in the college', a well, pump and cistern were installed.[10]

In his description of the pattern, Rich mentions the 'wonderful things wrought by the operation of the water'. Scientific tests of the water quality of Dublin springs by Dr Rutty during the middle of the eighteenth century noted that one of the 'wonderful' things wrought by the St Patrick's Well water was its laxative qualities. According to the doctor the water yielded:

> *from one hundred and ten, to two hundred grains of sediment from each gallon, which was chiefly marine salt and Nitre, as I have elsewhere shewn: and hence their laxative quality is to be derived.*[11]

Such a high level of salt must have made the water quite unpalatable, leading one writer to suggest that the well may have instigated the tradition of Irishmen 'drowning their shamrocks' on St Patrick's Day, requiring something [whiskey], to mask the 'cold and purgative' quality of the water.[12] An association between drunkenness and the activities around wells dedicated to St Patrick certainly appears to have been well-established from the seventeenth century, the phrase 'to have drunk at St Patrick's well' being a contemporary euphemism for drunkeness.[13]

Several rhymes and poems of the time also imply that not all activity around the well was of a strictly devotional nature. One, entitled *A Poem upon St Patrick's Well in 1716*, includes the lines:

> *These lines were found near Patrick's Well:*
> *When, or by whom, there's none can tell:*
> *But some pretend to say or think,*
> *'Twas by a Scholar, when in Drink;*
> *Not with that Water, to be sure,*
> *But that, he took, 'tis thought for Cure;*
> *And, when that he was sober grown,*
> *He writ the following of his own.*[14]

The well is also reputed to have been put to another slightly unorthodox use at the end of the seventeenth century when a doctor, variously identified as Sir Hans

Sloane[15] or Dr Gwither,[16] went to Liverpool, where he filled several barrels with the 'choicest spawn of frogs', a species which were at that time, reputedly not known in Ireland:

> *The doctor was a very ingenious physician, and a very good protestant: for which reason, to shew his zeal against popery, he placed some of the most promising spawn in the very fountain that is dedicated to the saint and known by the name of St Patrick's Well, where these animals had the impudence to make their first appearance. They have since this time very much increased and multiplied in the neighbourhood of that city. We have some curious enquirers into natural history, who observe their motions with a design to compute in how many years they will be able to hop from Dublin to Wexford: though as I am informed, not one of them has yet passed the mountains of Wicklow.[17]*

The well continued to play a significant role in the lives of Dubliners through to the early part of the eighteenth century, until 1729, when calamity struck and the spring ran dry. The cause is unclear, but this did not hamper speculation. The *Dublin Gazette* in late March of that year reported that it was either due to digging for stone too close to the well or

> *to the ill use that has been made of St Patrick's Day for some years past – but be that as it will, it could be wished everybody would take care to behave for the future as to prevent worse evil happening unto them.[18]*

Other commentators saw the hand of Saint Patrick himself at play, and in his satirical poem *On the sudden drying of St Patrick's Well, near Trinity College Dublin* Jonathan Swift suggested that the well had run dry as a demonstration of the Saint's displeasure with English governance:

> *Where is the holy well that bore my name?*
> *Fled to the fountain back, from whence it came!*
> *Fair freedom's emblem once, which smoothly*
> *And blessings equally on all bestows.*
> *Here from the neighbouring nursery of the arts,*
> *The students, drinking, raised their wit and parts;*
> *Here, for an age or more, improv'd their vein,*

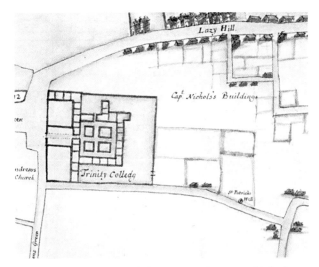

Fig. 2 – Bernard de Gomme, The Citty and Suburbs of Dublin (1673). Detail. © National Maritime Museum, London.

Their Phoebus I, my spring their Hippocrene.
Discouraged youths! Now all their hopes must fall,
Condemn'd to country cottages and ale;
To foreign prelates make a slavish court
And by their sweat procure mean support.[19]

Such was the popularity of the well still at this time that an appeal was made to the City Corporation to try to restore the flow of water. Two years later the *Dublin Weekly Journal* reported that

> *The water has again been restored to St Patrick's Well, to the very great satisfaction of the Inhabitants of this city, it has been dry for many months and is now again cleared up and repaired at the city charge, great complaints having been made about its loss.*[20]

Reference to the 'digging of stone' close to the well probably refers to use of the lands around the well at that time for development. Records of leases in the College registers confirm that the College owned the land, a portion of which was leased to a John White in the early eighteenth century.[21]   However, the Molesworths, the family responsible for laying out the area roughly bounded by Dawson Street, Nassau Street, Merrion Square and St Stephen's Green, showed a keen interest in the development of the 'St Patrick's Well Lands' from early in the century. In 1709 William Molesworth agreed with John White, who was presumably acting as his agent, to allow tenants in the cabins on St Patrick's Well Lands to extend their leases for another year, in the hope that adjacent developments by Joshua Dawson (who gave his name to Dawson Street), might improve the value of the land.[22] By 1724, Molesworth was still contemplating the 'setting out' of the Well Lands,[23] but correspondence with his brother, Viscount Robert, suggests that this was proving problematic due to the nature of his lease. In a letter of April 1728, Robert informed his brother that a strong argument had been made to have the new Parliament House located on the Well Lands. Due to the nature of his tenure, however, and the fact that two thousand pounds' worth of materials were already on the old site, this was unlikely to happen; but once a perpetual lease was secured, 'I am sure so fine a situate of ground will soon be laid out into a handsome building.'[24]

Fig. 3 – Henry Pratt, *Dublin* (1708). NLI 16 L 15.
© National Library of Ireland.

While a 'handsome building' does not seem to have materialised, the well itself does appear to have sunk into obscurity around this time. Seventeenth- and early eighteenth-century maps of the city, such as that by Bernard de Gomme (1673) (fig. 2) and a derivative map by Henry Pratt (1708) (fig. 3) show it prominently located and marked by a tower-like structure. In the more detailed survey by John Rocque of 1756, however, there is no sign of the well.

An important aspect of the well's representation in early maps is its location. Both de Gomme and Pratt show it located relatively far down St Patrick's Well Lane (now Nassau Street/ Leinster Street) on the College side. Two maps drawn up by the City Surveyor, John Green, in the 1680s of the area that now corresponds to the top of Grafton Street and Nassau Street described the latter as respectively 'High way from St Patrick's Well' and 'Way to St Patrick's Well', implying that the well lay at the end of the thoroughfare rather than near the top of it.[25] Indeed, the most likely location of the well, based on the collective evidence of pre-1730 maps,

Fig. 4 – Charles Brooking, *City and Suburbs of Dublin* (1728). Detail. NLI 16 9 49 (1). © National Library of Ireland.

is at the modern junction between Leinster Street and Lincoln Place. This is further reinforced by the unusual curve shown on the street at that point in Brooking's map of 1728 (fig. 4), which may have come about as a result of the presence of the well there.

There is no evidence in early maps of a well at the junction of Dawson and Nassau Streets, although by the nineteenth century this is one of the springs that had become known as St Patrick's Well. It was singled out as the original medieval spring by the noted Dublin historian J.T. Gilbert,[26] and also formed part of the setting for the novella *Ierne: A romance of St Patrick's Well, Trinity College,* published in 1895.[27]

In recent decades scholars have claimed that there were two, three and even four Saint Patricks, while some have claimed that he never existed at all.[28] A similar state of affairs existed for the well dedicated to the saint somewhere around Nassau Street in the nineteenth century, with three contenders for the dedication. A spring behind No. 9 Nassau Street, 'concealed in an ancient vault', was suggested by Edward Clibborn as the most likely candidate to be St Patrick's Well. The premises was occupied, from 1780, by Thompson's Steam Cutlery Works, who in an 1892 advertisement claimed that their business was located 'on the exact site of St Patrick's Well'.[29] Clibborn highlighted that the well behind No.15 Nassau Street had also historically been called St Patrick's Well in leases given by Simpson's Hospital, which gave rights to a number of houses in the locality to draw water from it.[30]

This is probably the same well that came to be utilised by the Cantrell and Cochrane plant established in Nassau Place in 1869 (fig. 5). Like their neighbours, Thompson's Steam Cutlery Works, they were keen to claim ownership of the well. As their business was the distribution and sale of mineral water, this was a key marketing asset, and was emphasised in their advertising. An extract from an 1892 Commercial Directory relates the following:

The water necessary for the purposes of manufacture is obtained from a well on the premises long known as St Patrick's Well. This splendid natural fount was for many years covered in, and it was only through Sir Henry Cochrane's indefatigable research into antiquarian and other sources that the well was discovered. This is situated immediately in the centre of the factory, the depth of the boring reaching a distance of 95 feet – 70 feet from the surface to the rock and 25 feet below the granite. The well is lined with cylinders from top to bottom, the water being elevated by two powerful steam pumps capable of lifting 2,000 gallons of water per hour and providing the most inexhaustible supply of the purest spring water for the purposes of the trade.[31]

When compared in the 1930s by an impartial disciple of St Patrick, the Cantrell and Cochrane water source was described as 'deep and gushing', of at least 96 feet in depth and 'springing as fresh as ever', while the Trinity well had 'no visible flow'.[32]

The presence of at least three wells along Nassau Street may be a symptom of the boom in Dublin development that coincided with a doubling of the capital's population between 1682 and 1722. Up to 1721 the city's water supply had been provided by the thirteenth-century reservoir fed by water from the River Poddle. By the early eighteenth century this was unable to meet the demands of the growing city, and work on establishing new waterworks was commenced, with householders paying corporation water rent collectors for the privilege of having a domestic water supply.[33] Costs were high, however, leading many householders to sink their own wells; indeed, it may well have been the sinking of new wells to serve recently erected houses along St Patrick's Well Lane that caused the holy well to dry up in 1729.

Prior to the construction of the current Provost's House Stables, the site was occupied by a range of Georgian houses and some outbuildings. On John Rocque's map of 1756, the location of the Trinity well is not marked, but coincides roughly with the boundary between a yard and a wooded area. At present, the most likely explanation for its origins would seem to be as a source of water for the houses which once occupied the stables site – a suggestion supported by the use of eighteenth-century brick in the construction of the well chamber. While most such domestic wells have long since been filled in, the preservation of this one may be attributable to its proximity to the Provost's stables, providing a free source of drinking water to those less concerned with issues of purity and taste.

While the current 'St Patrick's Well' is unlikely to be the original site of feast day revelries, it nevertheless preserves the memory of one of the most important focal

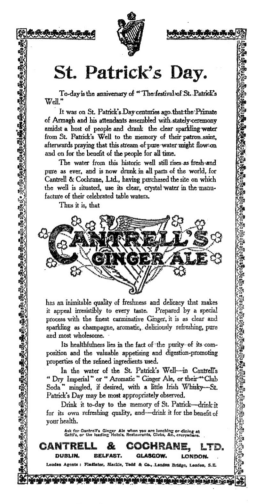

Fig. 5 – Cantrell and Cochrane advertisement. *The Times*, 17 March 1906.

points of Dublin life from the twelfth to the early eighteenth century. Its water supply may ultimately come from the same source as that of St Patrick's Well, but it now requires a good deal more than whiskey to make it potable.

[1]   'Extempore on the sudden death of an Irishman on St Patrick's Day', *The Western county magazine*, 3 (1789–92), p. 120.

[2]   Finglas, Boherboy, Jamestown, St Patrick's Close, Nassau Street and (doubtful) Skerries. Caoimhín Ó Danachair, 'The holy wells of County Dublin', *Reportorium Novum*, 2 (1958), pp 68–87.

[3]   Edmund L. Swift, *The life and acts of Saint Patrick* (Dublin, 1809), pp 95–6.

[4]   For the background to Jocelin's *Life* see Joseph Szövérffy, 'The Anglo-Norman conquest of Ireland and St Patrick', *Reportorium Novum*, 2 (1958), pp 6–16.

[5]   Richard Butler (ed.), *Registrum Prioratus Omnium Sanctorum Juxta Dublin* (Dublin, 1845), p. 94.

[6]   P.J. Corish, *The Catholic community in the seventeenth and eighteenth centuries* (Dublin, 1981), pp 50–1.

[7]   Barnabe Rich, *A new description of Ireland* (London, 1610), p. 52.

[8]   Barnabe Rich, *A Catholycke conference between Syr Thady Mac Mareall, a popish priest of Waterford and Patrick Playne, a young student of Trinity Colledge by Dublyne in Ireland* (London, 1612), p. 18.

[9]   TCD MS MUN/V/5/2, p. 84.

[10]   *Ibid.*, p. 101.

[11]   John Rutty, *An essay towards a natural, experimental and medicinal history of the mineral waters of Ireland* (Dublin, 1757), pp 18–19.

[12]   Edward Clibborn, *The Dublin water question: the springs of Dublin and fountains of Ath-Cliath and Dublinia attributed to St Patrick: proposed as an auxiliary to the present and any future supply of water to the city, with remarks, historical, statistical and economical, in relation to the further utilization of the Liffey Water* (Dublin, 1860), p. 26.

[13]   John Farmer and William Henley, *Slang and its analogues past and present. A dictionary, historical and comparative of the heterodox speech of all classes of society for more than three hundred years. With synonyms in English, French, German, Italian, etc.*, 7 vols. (1890–1904), VI, pp 93–4.

14   John Winstanley, *Poems written occasionally by John Winstanley... Interspers'd with many others, by several ingenious hands* (Dublin, 1742), pp 159–62.

15   *The Lubrications of Isaac Bickerstaff, esq.* 6 vols. (London, 1786), 6, pp 176–7.

16   T.P.C. Kirkpatrick, *History of the Medical School in Trinity College Dublin* (Dublin, 1912), pp 87–8.

17   *Bickerstaff*, 6, pp 176–7.

18   *The Dublin Gazette* (25–9 March, 1729), p. 185.

19   John Hawkesworth (ed.), *The works of Jonathan Swift, D.D. Dean of St. Patrick's, Dublin, accurately revised in six volumes, adorned with copper-plates* (London, 1775).

20   *Dublin Weekly Journal* (1731), 4: 22, p. 92.

21   TCD MS MUN/V/5/2, p. 503; TCD MSS MUN/V/5/3, pp 19, 81, 129.

22   Historic Manuscripts Commission, *Reports on manuscripts in various collections*, 7 (London, 1913), Clements MSS, p. 243.

23   *Ibid.*, p. 369.

24   *Ibid.*, p. 399.

25   Dublin City Archive, City Surveyor's Maps C1/S1/1; Dublin City Archives, Wide Streets Commissioners' Maps WSC/maps/565/1.

26   J.T. Gilbert, *History of the City of Dublin*, 3 vols. (Dublin, 1854), III, p. 244.

27   Mrs Thomas Alexander, *Ierne: A romance of St Patrick's Well, Trinity College* (Dublin, 1895).

28   A. Hopkin, *The living legend of Saint Patrick* (London, 1989), p. 151.

29   *Dublin, Cork and South of Ireland: a literary, commercial and social review of past and present* (London, 1892), p. 60.

30   Clibborn, *The Dublin water question*, p. 26.

31   *Dublin, Cork and South of Ireland*, p. 69.

32   Oliver St John Gogarty, *I follow St Patrick* (New York, 1938), pp 107–9.

33   Michael Corcoran, *Our good health: a history of Dublin's water and drainage* (Dublin, 2005), pp 11–14.

Fig. 1 – Michael Warren, *Go deo, homage to Samuel Beckett* (2006), bronze, height: 220 cm. Photo, Ros Kavanagh.

MICHAEL WARREN'S GO DEO, HOMAGE TO SAMUEL BECKETT

Yvonne Scott

But yesterday evening it was all black and bare. And now it's covered with leaves.
   – Vladimir, in *Waiting for Godot*, Act II.

Michael Warren's sculpture, *Go deo, homage to Samuel Beckett* (2006, fig. 1) is placed in the cobbled courtyard of the Provost's House Stables. As with all of this artist's work, the relationship to site has been carefully thought out, and, while conceived before its donation to this particular space, it has been placed and angled as though to point the way to the Irish Art Research Centre in its new home. This work represents also the intersection of both the writer and the artist with Trinity College: Beckett was a graduate in 1927, and subsequently taught here from 1930 to '31, while Michael Warren studied philosophy, psychology and English here in the early 1970s. *Go deo* is a homage from one of the most important Irish sculptors to one of the most important Irish writers of the last hundred years.

The Irish term *go deo*[1] (forever) plays on the French pronunciation of the title of Beckett's famous tragicomedy, *Waiting for Godot.*[2] The bronze sculpture appears to be a radical departure from the type of work for which Warren is most celebrated: the geometric, abstract, minimalist works made from enormous beams of solid wood, and assembled like giant constructivist puzzles that question and resolve issues of gravity and balance. *Countermovement* (1984–5, fig. 2), also in the College collection, is a prime example. Sited at the opposite end of the Trinity College campus, the work embodies a rational, ordered aesthetic and is located, appropriately, it might be argued, near the science and engineering quarters. It is constructed of timber, and has no obvious literal content. By contrast, *Go deo* presents itself as the diametric opposite: it is made of bronze and includes a mimetic element that is rare in Warren's oeuvre – a gnarled branch twists around its supporting, somewhat abstract, cross-shaped structure (fig. 3). The elements of branch and of cut timber are created not by modelling, however, but by casting directly from wood, thereby blurring the boundaries between reality and illusion, and between original and copy.

Michael Warren's Go deo, homage to Samuel Beckett *was donated to Trinity College Dublin in 2006 by David Arnold to mark the centenary of the birth of Samuel Beckett (1906–1988). The location, in the stableyard of the Provost's House Stables, was proposed by Prof. David Spearman, Fellow Emeritus, Trinity College Dublin.*

Fig. 2 – Michael Warren, *Countermovement* (1984–85), Spanish chestnut, 117 x 330 x 428 cm. Photo, Michael Warren.

Opposite: *Fig. 3* – Michael Warren, *Go deo, homage to Samuel Beckett* (detail) 2006, bronze, height: 220 cm. Photo, Ros Kavanagh.

Because Warren's work is typically non-figurative, while the material and organic quality of the wood in examples like *Countermovement* are always paramount, it presents itself primarily as timber, with its origin as a tree disguised by the functionality of the constituent beams. *Go deo*, paradoxically, while made of bronze, asserts its inherent quality as a tree. Appropriately, the model from which it has been cast was made from a variety of woods sourced in Ireland; the base is oak, the stem is elm, and the horizontal element is made from sycamore. In deference to the text of the play, and to the aesthetic of the tree itself, the branch configuration is cast from willow:

ESTRAGON : (*Looking at the tree*). *What is it?*

VLADIMIR : *It's the tree.*

ESTRAGON: *Yes, but what kind?*

VLADIMIR: *I don't know. A willow.*

– *Waiting for Godot*, Act I

As the single element of 'scenery', the tree is typically presented in stage productions as stunted, misshapen, and/or flimsy, and its role has been variously interpreted. While it is argued that Beckett did not intend it as a symbol, at least not in a specific or prescriptive way, it nonetheless carries a range of associations, some of which are suggested by the text. Most commentators on the play identify biblical connotations;[3] the Tree of Knowledge in Genesis, significantly, marked the origins of human frailty, and the wooden cross of the Crucifixion represented for Beckett not so much the salvation of man as the tortuous nature of his existence.

Warren points out that the tree of the play was not intended as a functional stage prop, but indicates its complex role:

> Does it depict the Tree of Knowledge/of Life, a hangman's gibbet, a cross, a crown of thorns… or is it after all just some sort of 'bush'?[4]

He qualifies this comment by reference to the inability of the play's characters to decide on whether it is a tree, a shrub or a bush, a factor that clearly indicates its relatively diminutive scale.

There are precedents in the representation by artists of Beckett's 'tree'. However, while Warren's work is intended as an independent sculpture, some artists were commissioned to produce the stage prop itself, the most famous of which was by Beckett's friend, the sculptor Alberto Giacometti.[5] Warren explains that Giacometti's 'interpretation is at once symbolic, surreal and deliberately ambivalent. So too, *Go deo* remains open to a number of interpretations.'[6] A clue to a reading of the dominant cruciform shape of Warren's interpretation is his familiarity with the idea that the names of the two main protagonists in the play, Vladimir and Estragon, are 'reputedly references to Vladimir the Russian saint on

the one hand, and on the other, estragon, a plant botanically belonging to the family *cruciferae*'.[7] Such religious connotations are unavoidable, and Beckett was certainly familiar with the implications, given his upbringing by a mother noted for her religious devotion, his own stated familiarity and intention to use it, together with his possession of biblical concordances.[8] When Estragon removes his boots, and Vladimir comments in Act II that he cannot go barefoot, Estragon retorts 'Christ did!'; he goes on to point out that he has always compared himself to Christ and makes reference to the Crucifixion.

The theme of the Crucifixion has recurred in Warren's work, subtly presented in the occasional, abstract, 'triptych' pieces, and culminating in the installation exhibition in 2007 at the Royal Hibernian Academy, *Of Weight and Wings*, which drew elements of the series together with a major new work, collectively making reference to Andrea Mantegna's *Calvary* of 1450 (figs. 4 and 5). In visual art, the narrative sequence surrounding the Crucifixion traditionally includes a partially dead tree that also demonstrates signs of life, with sprouting leaves and branches – signifying the end of the old dispensation, and the new order heralded by Christianity. In *Waiting for Godot*, there are references to new leaves, and Vladimir comments: 'Everything is dead but the tree'. However, any interpretation of hope and the future has apparently been refuted by Beckett, who indicated that the leaves were intended simply to signify the passing of time and therefore the very nature of existence. Leaves are indicative of seasonal cycles, and spring is referred to in that

Fig. 4 – (Top left) Michael Warren, *Piazza* (2007), painted MDF, 40 x 1150 x 1150 cm. Photo, Donal Murphy.

Fig. 5 – (Above) Michael Warren, *Triptychos* (1982–84), oak and forged iron, 150 x 150 x 20 cm. Photo, Donal Murphy.

context, while references in the play to the sun and the moon, and to sunrise and sunset, indicate the relentless passing of the days. Leaves are mentioned in the dialogue in relation, also, to sand and to ashes, clear references to time and to death. This element is suggested also by Warren's title 'forever', with all its various temporal implications. His tree is noticeably barren, placing it early in the unfolding of the play. Warren's work has other temporal elements, to do with the time it takes to cross a space. The linear, horizontal qualities of the longer arm indicate, for Warren, duration and therefore the passage of time, and it has been read as a signpost pointing the direction.[9] There is the element of the inferred journey: the base of the structure has been likened to a mounting block – appropriate in the context of the Provost's House Stables.

Notwithstanding the lack of a functional role for the tree in the play, there are attempts in the dialogue to make use of it: to hide behind it and, in the final lines, for the protagonists to hang themselves from it. The latter project is abandoned, however, for lack of a rope, but the irony resides in the patent unsuitability of the tree to successfully facilitate either of these possibilities of 'disappearance'. Denied the means to absent themselves, time moves relentlessly on for them.

The ambiguity of the play, described by the *New York Times* in 1956 as 'a mystery wrapped in an enigma', is, of course, part of its attraction and continued fascination.[10] For all its apparent bleakness, the text on which Warren's work is based evokes a wry humour, and the play itself has sparked endless debate over its potential meaning. The relationship between art and text is the basis of art history, which depends on language to record, describe, analyse and debate the nature of the image. Interestingly, it was a painting that prompted Beckett to write his play. He explained that it was based on Casper David Friedrich's *Man and Woman Contemplating the Moon* (1824)[11]. Warren's sculpture, in turn, is the progeny of Beckett's text. The juxtaposition in *Go deo* of the literal and the abstract, realism and illusion, nature and art, in a work that addresses both the immediacy of the present, and the boundlessness of the infinite, is entirely appropriate as a pointer to the Centre.

1   Pronounced 'guh djo'.

2   *Waiting for Godot* was written by Samuel Beckett in 1948, in French. The first public performance took place in 1953, and it was first performed in English in 1955. The version of the text consulted for this essay was: Samuel Beckett, *Waiting for Godot, a tragicomedy* (London, 2004).

3   There are numerous instances; see for example, Anthony Cronin, *Samuel Beckett, the last modernist* (London, 1997), pp 20–21.

4   Correspondence from Michael Warren to Yvonne Scott, 28 Dec. 2006.

5   See Riann Coulter, 'Introduction to the exhibition: part 2' in National Gallery of Ireland, *Samuel Beckett: A passion for painting*, exhibition cat. (Dublin, 2006), pp 22–33.

6   Correspondence, 28 Dec. 2006.

7   *Ibid.*

8   Cronin, *Samuel Beckett*, p. 21.

9   Correspondence from Michael Warren to Yvonne Scott, 16 and 17 Feb. 2008.

10 Brooks Atkinson, 'Beckett's "Waiting for Godot"', *New York Times*, 20 April 1956.

11 James Knowlson, *Damned to fame: The life of Samuel Beckett* (London, 1996), p. 378. Apparently Beckett had suggested elsewhere that it was based on an almost identical painting by Friedrich, *Two Men Contemplating the Moon* (1819).

CONTRIBUTORS

Desmond FitzGerald, the Knight of Glin is Doctor in Letters (*honoris causa*) of Trinity College Dublin. He is President of the Irish Georgian Society and a Director of the Castletown Foundation, the Irish Landmark Trust and the Irish Heritage Trust. He is also a Governor of the National Gallery of Ireland. His publications include *Ireland's Painters* (2002) with Anne Crookshank, and *Irish Furniture* (2007) with James Peill (both published by Yale University Press). He is the author of numerous other books and articles on Irish architecture and the decorative arts. At present he is working on the history of the FitzGeralds of Glin with contributions by a number of historians.

Patricia McCarthy is research assistant at the Irish Art Research Centre (TRIARC) and is currently pursuing a PhD at Trinity College entitled 'The planning and use of space in country and town houses in Ireland, 1730–1830'. The author of *A favourite study: building the King's Inns* (Gill & Macmillan, 2006), she has published articles in the *Irish Arts Review Yearbook*, *Irish Architectural and Decorative Studies* and in *Country Life*.

Edward McParland is a lecturer in the Department of the History of Art, and Fellow, at Trinity College Dublin. He is co-founder (with Nicholas Robinson), and former Chairman, of the Irish Architectural Archive. Among his representations, he served on the Committee of Management of the Irish Georgian Foundation for many years. His research interests include Irish architecture from the seventeenth to nineteenth centuries, and problems in architectural classicism. His publications include *James Gandon*, *Vitruvius Hibernicus* (Zwemmer, 1985), and *Public Architecture in Ireland 1680-1760* (Yale University Press, 2001).

Rachel Moss is a lecturer and archives manager in the Irish Art Research Centre (TRIARC). She has published a number of articles on medieval art and architecture and edited/ co-edited two books, *Art and Devotion in Late Medieval Ireland* (Four Courts Press, 2006) and *Making and Meaning in Insular Art* (Four Courts Press, 2007).

Yvonne Scott is Director of the Irish Art Research Centre (TRIARC). She has published on various aspects of modern and contemporary art, particularly Irish, including (as editor) *Jack Yeats: Old and New Departures* (Four Courts Press, 2008). Exhibitions curated, with accompanying catalogues, include *Patrick Scott: A Retrospective* (Hugh Lane Gallery, 2002), and *The West as Metaphor* (Royal Hibernian Academy, 2005). Forthcoming books address, respectively, the work of Patrick Ireland/Brian O'Doherty, and agendas in landscape imagery.

John Tuomey is a graduate of UCD School of Architecture. He established his partnership with Sheila O'Donnell in 1988 with the Irish Film Institute as their first public commission. O'Donnell+Tuomey have won more than forty national and international awards in twenty years of practice, including the RIAI Gold Medal awarded for the Ranelagh School. They represented Ireland at the Venice Biennale in 2004. Current projects include the Pearse Street Development Plan for Trinity College, Photographers' Gallery London and Lyric Theatre Belfast. He is author of *Architecture, Craft and Culture*, published by Gandon Editions, 2004.